"Now That Time Has Had Its Say":

A History of the Indianapolis Central Canal

1835—2002

by

J. Darrell Bakken

ISBN: 1-4033-3911-2 (e-book)
ISBN: 1-4033-3912-0 (Paperback)

This book is printed on acid free paper.

Library of Congress Control Number: 2002092363

Printed in the United States of America
Bloomington, IN

1stBooks – rev. 12/2/02

TABLE OF CONTENTS

now that time has had its say

Time the runner has swiftly passed us by.
We wonder if the water still flows
Through the City.

We've heard it doesn't,
That now on super highways
Automobiles dash in and out,
Taking up the water course.

Some historical archaeologists
Can probably discern why the Canal was built,
From where it took its water
And where it flowed,
of what use it was.

We knew it started out north.
We walked the path alongside
That horses toiled to draw the boats.

We thought that the quiet stream
Could have use for canoes and parasols
Like a painting by Degas.

Of course such dreams came to naught.
The city planners had to accommodate
The gas burners.

Since I stayed near the Canal for many years,
I thought it took on a spiritual meaning.
Now that Time has had its say,
I wonder if anyone else remembers.

Courtesy O. James Fox and Indiana Historical Society

PREFACE AND ACKNOWLEDGMENTS

The relationship between the Indianapolis Water Company (a public water supply utility founded in 1881), the controversial Indiana Central Canal (constructed between 1836 and 1839), and the city of Indianapolis that they have jointly served since 1881 includes many previously unpublished stories that deserve to be told.

As I waded through the extensive Indianapolis Water Company (IWC) archives, as well as numerous newspaper articles, governmental and legal documents, and canal histories dating back to 1835, I discovered a 120-year story in which a private company and a city, through joint stewardship and dedication, turned the Central Canal financial disaster of the 1830s into the Water Company Canal of today—a valuable asset to the company and a priceless city and state historical treasure.

The depth and breadth of this book are possible primarily because of the historical interest of many past and present IWC employees, in particular three public relations professionals: John Kleinhenz, Pat Chastian, and George Bredewater. They, along with other colleagues, placed and maintained in the company archives an enormous volume of canal histories, articles, press releases, brochures, memos, photographs, and legal documents. The volume of material was so great that it required twenty-five months for me to collect, digest, summarize, and write about it.

Thanks to company officers Jim Morris, Joe Broyles, Dave Kelly, Ken Giffin, Tim Bumgardner, John Davis, and Bob Miller for their support.

Many thanks for the assistance and advice of retirees Paul Doane, Tom Beaven, Maury Stout, Steve Lyons, Walter Meehan, Dan Morse, and, before his untimely death, Bob Becker.

Thanks also to employees who willingly assisted with research, photocopying, scanning, and other tasks—Jim Gunn, Virginia Wilson, Tom Dougherty, Charline Avey, Duane Whiting, Wanda

Wooldridge, and Mike Witte.

I appreciate receiving ready access to the files of the Indiana State Library, the Indiana Historical Society, the Indiana Historic Landmarks Foundation, the Indianapolis Department of Metropolitan Development (Real Estate Services and Historic Preservation), the Indianapolis—Marion County Public Library, and Butler University Library. Current and former DMD employees Larry Coffey, Paula Whitney, Harold Rominger, Steve Schulmeyer, and Mike Perry were very helpful. Thanks to Susan Sutton and Wilma Gibbs of the IHS and to Mindi Woolman of Historic Landmarks.

Baker & Daniels attorneys Fred Schlegel and Ben Blanton, and Tom Lofton, now with Lilly Endowment, provided important information on the canal's legal history.

Members of the Indiana Canal Society, particularly Chuck Huppert and Professor Ralph Gray, were extremely helpful with my research on the early Central Canal.

One hundred thanks to my wife, Ruth Bakken, for keeping me on the long and winding two-year path to completing this project. And one thousand thanks to daughter Dawn Bakken for typing the book's many drafts and for transforming my technical jargon into historical prose. Profound thanks also to Nancy Zeilig, former editor of the American Water Works Association Journal, for her insightful editing.

Although several publications on what was originally the Indiana Central Canal are available, most of them contain discrepancies in basic data (such as the overall length of the canal). In this work, I have relied whenever possible on data from primary sources—deed abstracts, official plats and surveys, and signed engineering reports—and have used modern measurements to clear up discrepancies. What follows is a technical and corporate history written by a water resources engineer with a deep interest in history.

J. Darrell Bakken
Indianapolis, Indiana
May 2002

INDIANA'S CANALS

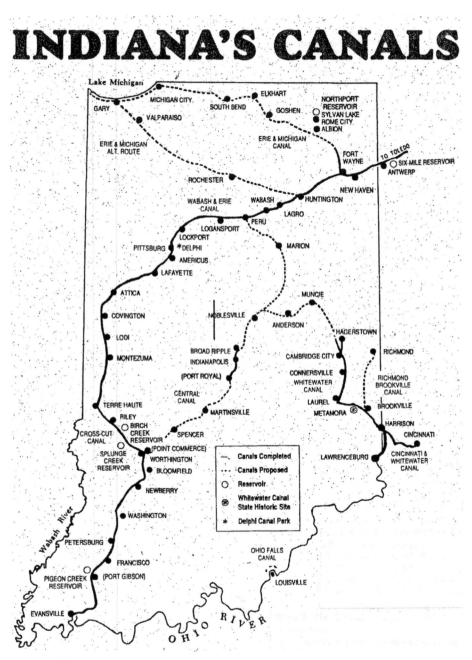

Courtesy CSI

x

THE CENTRAL CANAL

This map shows one hundred eighty-five miles of the Central Canal from Peru, Indiana to Point Commerce (Worthington), Indiana. Below Point Commerce the Central Canal continued 111 miles to Evansville and eventually became a part of the Wabash & Erie Canal. The total length of the Central Canal if it had been built as planned would have been 296 miles.

Map by Charles Huppert, October 1999.

Indiana Central Canal

Courtesy Chuck Huppert

CENTRAL CANAL

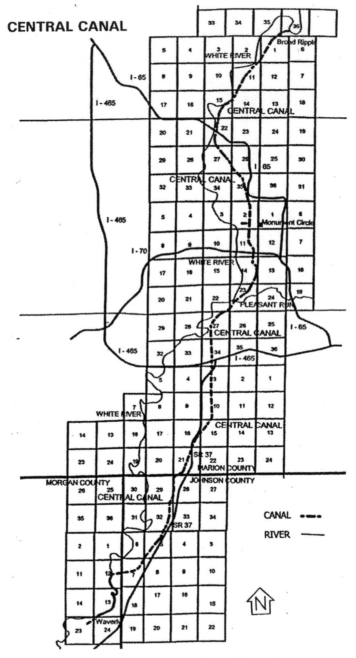

2002 computer map of the Central Canal's route

Courtesy WTH Engineering

PROLOGUE
AN OVERVIEW OF THE CANAL'S HISTORY

The story of the Central Canal begins in Indianapolis in 1835, only fourteen years after the city was laid out in 1821 and forty-six years before creation of the Indianapolis Water Company. The canal was one of eight projects authorized by the Internal Improvements Bill passed by the Indiana General Assembly in 1836. According to historian Paul Fatout, the bill authorized eight improvement projects, including a Central Canal "from the Wabash River between Ft. Wayne and Logansport, via Muncietown and Indianapolis, then down White River to Evansville." The legislature appropriated $3.5 million for the canal project and authorized state commissioners to borrow $10 million over twenty-five years for all eight projects. The legislature also authorized building 25 miles of the Central Canal "extending from the feeder dam above Indianapolis [Broad Ripple] to the Bluffs [at Port Royal]." The line of the canal as described in the legislation took in "a Dam across the White river, an Aqueduct over Fall creek, 8 Lift Locks, most of which will be built of cut stone, 2 or 3 Bluff sections, and several large Culverts."[1]

Fatout describes this Hoosier scheme of internal improvements as "conceived in madness and nourished by delusion," noting that the yearly interest on a $10 million loan at the stated interest rate of 5 percent would have been $500,000, or ten times Indiana's revenues from taxation. Fatout also observed that the Improvements Act "provided no means of paying the interest."[2]

State engineers completed the route survey for the new canal during the summer of 1835. A little more than three years later, on June 27, 1839, the state diverted water into the operational part of the Central Canal and placed it into service with appropriate political and public ceremony. The operational portion of the canal extended 13 miles (with the addition of a half-mile mill race) from Broad Ripple to Pleasant Run Creek, near what is now the intersection of West Street (Bluff Road) and Southern Avenue. The remaining 7 miles in southern Marion County and 5½ miles in

Johnson County from the Marion County line to the Bluffs at Port Royal were not operational after June 1839. The state ran out of money to build aqueducts or culverts over Pleasant Run Creek and four other creeks between Pleasant Run and Port Royal, and without them there was no possibility of furnishing a continuous Canal water supply for that lower portion.[3]

From 1839 to 1851 the state of Indiana owned and operated the 13-mile Central Canal from Broad Ripple to Pleasant Run Creek and the half-mile mill race from Market and Missouri Streets west and south to White River between Washington and Maryland Streets. The state's first use of the canal was to lease its water power to companies located adjacent to the canal and mill race, including a woolen mill, a cotton mill, a linseed oil mill, two gristmills, two sawmills, and two paper mills. The canal's other early use was for transportation between downtown Indianapolis and Broad Ripple, both for business and for pleasure. By 1850, however, the annual cost of canal operation and maintenance greatly exceeded the income from canal water use, and the state authorized sale of the Central Canal to the highest bidder.

In June 1851 the state sold the northern division of the canal (the portion north of the Morgan County line) to the Indiana Central Canal Manufacturing, Hydraulic and Water Works Company of Rochester, New York. Water was never diverted through the 12½ miles of constructed canal from Pleasant Run Creek through Marion and Johnson counties to the Morgan County boundary, and this stretch of the canal had apparently been abandoned before 1851. The 1851 owner deeded the canal title to the Indiana Central Canal Company in March 1864, and that New York company, on May 1, 1870, sold the canal to the Water Works Company of Indianapolis (WWCI). Both companies, like the state before them, produced minimal income from the canal in the face of much greater maintenance expenses.

During the 1860s, six attempts (two in 1860, and one in 1864, 1865, 1866, and 1868) were made to form a public water supply utility for Indianapolis. Most of these proposals suggested using the Central Canal for water supply or pumping (both believed to be financially promising uses for canal water). All of these attempts occurred prior to a January 3, 1870, city ordinance authorizing the WWCI to design, construct, operate, and maintain a public water supply system within one year and five months. In May 1871, the Indianapolis *Journal* recorded that "On and after Thursday, June 1, 1871 [seventeen months after passage of the ordinance], the machinery of the Water Works Company of Indianapolis, will be run day and night for supplying the city and citizens with water."[4]

In 1870 the WWCI acquired a city council charter and ownership of the 13-mile Central Canal and the half-mile mill race for a reported sum of $200,000. During the ensuing seventeen months, the company invested great effort and perhaps as much as $500,000 for a well-water supply, a pumping station (on West Washington Street at White River), and a few miles of cast-iron water mains. Despite these investments, however, few customers gave up their private wells and connected to the utility in its first ten years, and industrial use of the canal also declined.

In 1881 the new Indianapolis Water Company (IWC) successfully bid $500,000 to acquire the $1.4 million-plus assets of the WWCI at a sheriff's sale on the county courthouse steps. A few years earlier, in 1873, approximately 4.7 miles of the Central Canal south of Market Street had been sold to a railroad and abandoned. Thus, when the IWC purchased all of the WWCI's assets, it acquired only 8.3 miles of the canal—from the White River at Broad Ripple south to Missouri and Market streets—and the half-mile mill race.

IWC initiated several new recreational uses for the canal. Then in 1904 the company began what became the second principal use of the canal's water supply—gravity conveyance of raw water from Broad Ripple south to a new water treatment plant. From a financial standpoint, the most significant use of the canal from 1923 through the 1940s came from its replacement cost value, which constituted a substantial portion of the utility's overall rate valuation.

Since the 1970s the lower portion of the canal has served a very different function as part of the redevelopment of Indianapolis's downtown business district. An investment of at least $70 million of government and foundation funds has helped to spur more than $190 million of private and nonprofit development along the restored canal east and north of the West Street Bridge. West of the bridge, there are now three major museums and the restored Washington Station Pump House, representing more than $210 million of additional public and private investment in the future of Indianapolis.[5]

CHAPTER 1
INDIANA CONSTRUCTS THE CENTRAL CANAL

In 1815 the Indiana Territorial Assembly and Governor Thomas Posey obtained the approval of the United States Congress to transform Indiana from a territory into a state. Indiana joined the union in 1816. State delegates met in the old territorial capital of Corydon on June 10, 1816, to draft a constitution, which was officially approved June 27.

Indianapolis becomes the new state's capital

Corydon was declared the capital of the new state, but discussions about transferring the capital to a more central location began by 1818. The legislature created a ten-member commission to locate an appropriate site in the center of the new state, which had been cleared of Indian titles by federal treaties. Lack of settlement in this part of Indiana meant that the state government could own land in the new capital, a fact that would be significant in the location and acquisition of land for the Central Canal almost twenty years later. The commission held its first meeting May 22, 1820, at the home of pioneer settler William Conner on the banks of the White River just south of present-day Noblesville. In determining a location for the new capital, the group considered sites on both sides of the White River all the way from Noblesville south to the bluffs of Waverly. They chose a site on the east bank of the White River at the original junction with Fall Creek. The new capital, called Indianapolis, was platted in 1821 by Lieutenant Governor Christopher Harrison, Alexander Ralston, and Elias P. Fordham. The town was a one-mile square, with the White River and Fall Creek junction situated about half a mile west of the west line of the plat.[6]

The state government needed funds to erect public buildings in its new capital, and the sale of state-owned lots began October 8,

1821. Real estate advertisements claimed many positive attributes for the lots, including the fact that "Good wholesome water may be had at the depth of 26 feet, in any part of [the lots], in a sandy stratum."[7]

Marion County and its townships were created in 1822. The state assembly did not, however, simultaneously authorize town government for Indianapolis, another important factor one decade later in the acquisition of land for the Central Canal.

Canal fever spreads to Indiana

By the mid-1820s, what state historian Donald Carmony characterized as "a serious, persistent and incurable case of internal improvement fever" had gripped the imaginations of many Hoosier leaders. Indiana was following the rest of the country, where internal improvement schemes—including roads, bridges, canals, and later railroads—were becoming a national passion.[8]

Canal fever in Indiana owed much of its fervor to the success of the Erie Canal in upper New York state. Canals were already reaching from the East into the midwestern frontier: the Erie Canal connected New York state's interior with Pennsylvania and Ohio (via Lake Erie), and the Maumee River Canal connected Lake Erie with the Indiana state line (via Ohio). The first major construction project within Indiana was the Wabash and Erie Canal, which eventually extended from the Maumee Valley at the state line to Fort Wayne, along the Wabash River from Fort Wayne to Terre Haute, from Terre Haute to Worthington, and from there to Evansville and the Ohio River.[9]

The diary of Calvin Fletcher, a prominent nineteenth-century Hoosier businessman, sheds light on Indiana's passion to build canals. In an August 1835 entry, Fletcher recorded a meeting with Governor Noah Noble. Both men agreed that canals were a good investment for a state—better than railroads—because all the money spent on canals remained in the state, whereas half to two thirds of the investment in a railroad would leave the state through

2

the purchase of rails and equipment. Fletcher pronounced the idea of a canal from Indianapolis north to the Wabash River "certainly practicable" but expressed doubts about building a canal from Indianapolis all the way south to the Ohio River.[10]

Indiana authorizes construction of the Central Canal

The Internal Improvements Act of the 1836 Indiana General Assembly authorized eight large transportation projects and gave the state's canal commissioners authority to borrow $10 million at 5 percent interest over twenty-five years to pay for construction. One of these projects was the Central Canal, which was to connect with the Wabash and Erie Canal at the Wabash River between Wabash and Peru; run via the Mississinewa River and Pipe Creek to the White River near Anderson; and then run along the White River to Indianapolis, Waverly, and Worthington, where it would rejoin the Wabash and Erie and go across country to Evansville. The cost of the canal was estimated at $3.5 million. The legislation's description of the construction of 25 miles of the Central Canal from the feeder dam on the White River at Broad Ripple through Indianapolis to the bluffs at Port Royal indicated that the project was to include the feeder dam, a Fall Creek aqueduct, eight lift locks, two or three bluff sections, and several large culverts.[11]

The survey to locate the line of the canal had already been authorized by the general assembly in February 1835. According to the annual reports of the state canal commissioners and their engineers, the entire 290-mile center-line survey of the Central Canal was completed that summer. The surveyed line of the canal began at the Wabash and Erie Canal at the mouth of the Mississinewa River and ended at the Ohio River at Evansville. William Gooding surveyed the canal's route north of downtown Indianapolis; Francis Cleveland surveyed the route south of Indianapolis to Evansville. Both surveys were conducted under the supervision of state canal engineer Jesse Lynch Williams.[12]

General Thomas A. Morris, a noted Indiana engineer, businessman, and public servant (and future president of the Indianapolis Water Company) recalled the second construction survey in an 1898 interview:

> I located the line of this canal, laid it off and superintended the construction. I surveyed the line from Wabashtown to Martinsville. It went through a rather rough country. I camped out for six months, but came into town for Christmas. Many a morning we had to shake the snow off ourselves when we got up.
>
> There were forests and thickets and a great deal of swampy ground. There was a big swamp a mile or so south of Broad Ripple which contained water nearly all the year, and was a great feeding place for wild ducks. There was another big swamp southeast of this, near Hiram Bacon's place on the Noblesville road, west to the river. Remains of the former swamp still exist. I have had some good sport shooting snipes and ducks there.

Morris's statements indicate that, as canal engineer, he conducted the construction survey "from Wabashtown to Martinsville" to specify width, depth, and other canal dimensions and then supervised construction of the Central Canal portions actually completed from Anderson to Broad Ripple, from the Broad Ripple dam through Indianapolis to the Port Royal bluffs, and south of Waverly to Martinsville.[13]

The state assembles the land for the canal

In 1836 the state of Indiana owned the vast majority of the land upon which the new canal would be built. Within the mile-square of Indianapolis, the state owned all unsold land; outside the square it owned all the land from Broad Ripple south to Wellington. Even the streets of Indianapolis had not been given over to the town government's control, but were owned by the state.

Within the town of Indianapolis, land acquisition occurred piece by piece. The canal route entered the platted mile-square of Indianapolis at what is now the intersection of West 10th and Fayette Streets. About 1,000 feet of canal right-of-way was acquired from private parties from that point to Missouri Street at St. Clair. The state, by resolution of the Board of Internal Improvements, took possession of Missouri Street from St. Clair to Merrill Street. From there the canal route proceeded southeast through private property, then south and southwest and south again to Pleasant Run Creek (at what is now the intersection of Bluff Road and Southern Street), and finally ran mostly south through the rest of Marion County and into northwestern Johnson County to the Port Royal bluffs.

The state also acquired land for an east-west crosscut arm—for the mill race and flume—at right angles to the line of the canal. The mill race, with water flow controlled by a stone lock at Missouri and Market Streets, was built to furnish water to industries that would use water wheels for their power source. To encourage factories to locate along the canal, the state set aside a seven-acre land tract known as the Steam Mill Lot, and purchased a future mill site (the block immediately south of the mill race) from the town. The state also purchased a tract it called the "Reserve," which extended two blocks west of the future mill site for another mill race.

At the west edge of the Reserve the state purchased a five-acre tract to build a two-level mill race basin. The east-west crosscut arm discharged into an upper-level mill race which extended south to mills and north to a spillway which could convey water to a lower-level mill race, running south and west into White River.[14]

Construction begins in 1836

Construction on the Central Canal from Broad Ripple to the Port Royal bluffs began in October 1836. The Broad Ripple feeder dam and the canal inlet from the White River were located just north of the current intersection of East 62nd Street and Westfield Boulevard.[15] The original feeder dam on White River, still in use today, was described as a timber, rock, and earth-filled dam 8 feet high and 300 feet long. The dam's foundation, excavated 3½ feet below the low water level, was filled to low water level with brush and uncut trees. Workers held the fill in place by laying the crib work and filling the cribs with stone. Backwater behind the dam extended four miles upstream and was confined by levees. The state owned the land under the water in White River and on both sides of the river from the feeder dam to a point north.[16]

Contractor John Burke directed construction of the first portion of the Indianapolis and Northern divisions of the canal from Broad Ripple to the Port Royal bluffs. The canal began at a point on the west bank of the White River between the separate communities of Broad Ripple and Wellington. At that time the only connection between Broad Ripple and Indianapolis was a single dirt road, known as Range Line Road, through the wilderness. All of the land north of what is now 10th Street in Indianapolis to the west edge of Broad Ripple was uninhabited and heavily forested. First, workers had to clear the canal route of trees and stumps; then they used shovels and picks to excavate the route about 6 feet deep and 60 feet wide. They loaded the dirt into wagons and hauled it to the sides to be used for the canal's banks and towpath. The labor-intensive work required about 750 men, by reports mostly Irish and German. Construction work in the forested and swampy wilderness was hard; perhaps one in six of the workers died.[17] Laborers in Evansville on the southern division of the canal earned $20 per month. Burke's workers in Broad Ripple were also compensated with seven 1½-ounce jiggers of whisky per day, handed out at regular intervals by the whisky boss.[18]

An early twentieth-century typescript in the Indianapolis Water Company's archives gives further details.[19]

Construction of the Indianapolis Division of the Central Canal proceeded during the year 1837 and to the fall of the year 1838 by which time the credit of the state was almost exhausted. The canal was completed [and watered] from Broad Ripple into and through the City of Indianapolis [to Pleasant Run], a stone lock having been built at the junction of the main canal and crosscut canal and another lock having been constructed about two miles south of that point for the development of power for a mill.[20] As the money then available by the state for construction work was exhausted the contracts remaining open were rescinded and all work was stopped. Such part of the canal as had been completed was then available for navigation, but comparatively little use was made of it for that purpose except in bringing lumber and farm products from Broad Ripple to Indianapolis.[21]

The state built a boat basin in downtown Indianapolis for both canal barges and excursion boats; it was on the east side of the canal between Market and Washington streets (where state office buildings are now located). Another boat basin was located south of Washington Street and east of the canal, extending east to Tennessee Street (now Capitol Avenue), south to Maryland Street, and west again to the canal.

The 1838 and 1839 reports of the state canal engineers claim that construction of the Indianapolis Division of the Central Canal was completed through Marion and Johnson counties all the way from Broad Ripple to the Port Royal bluffs, except for the framework of the nine wooden locks between south Indianapolis and Port Royal. According to the 1839 Indianapolis Division report, the canal was first filled with water from Broad Ripple to Indianapolis during that year, and later that summer it was filled to a point six miles below Market Street. The remainder of the canal, the report said, could be filled at any time desired. The Port Royal dam, 9 feet above low water and 395 feet long, was also reported to be complete. Through 1839, the cost of the canal for "a distance of 24 miles 58 chains" (24.725 miles) was "estimated at $435,496, not including the (wood) frame work of locks. Of this sum $434, 716 has been estimated to contractors."[22]

A decade later the state auditor's report of 1848 listed the costs of the "N. Division of Central Canal" as $882,088.93. Deducting the cost of the Indianapolis Division of the canal from this total leaves $446,593 as the cost of the northern portion of the canal from the Wabash and Erie Canal to Anderson and Broad Ripple. These latter construction costs were not recovered, because the same auditor's report lists the sum of the tolls received by the entire Northern Division of the Central Canal as $15,008.76. Canal operation and maintenance took all of these funds and more.

Canal is used for navigation and water-wheel power

The state developed two uses for the partially completed Central Canal: navigation—by means of freight barges and excursion boats pulled by horses—and water-wheel power, using the flow of the White River diverted by the Broad Ripple Dam and the amount of head, or fall, in the canal from the dam to downtown Indianapolis. In his study of the canal, Robert C. Earle discussed both of these uses:

When the Central Canal opened in 1839, woolen mills, cotton mills, paper mills and sawmills were erected along the route to utilize the water power. For years the major industries of Indianapolis were centered around this water power development. The annual growth of grass, or the breaking of the canal banks, however (largely due to muskrats), proved the canal not efficient enough for such usage. Mills, however, still used the canal to transport their goods. One packet, the "Silver Bell," made regular runs transporting cord wood and people. The boat was painted silver and was hung with silver bells. Silver-grey mules wearing silver harnesses pulled the boat at an average speed of 8 miles per hour[23] A trip on the Silver Bell was considered the height of good living.

An enterprising young man named Robert Earl ... started a line of sight-seeing canal boats running on scheduled times between Indianapolis and Broad Ripple. He advertised his business in the Indianapolis newspapers.

The Canal Boat
Now running on the canal between Indianapolis and the Broad Ripple will ply daily. The boat leaves Indianapolis at ten o'clock in the morning, and returns at six o'clock in the evening. Good order will at all times be maintained on the boat and every attention paid to render those comfortable who may take passage. Fare $1. Persons visiting the Broad Ripple are assured that good entertainment will be found by those desiring eatables, etc.
Robert Earl[24]

Earle's account of his great-great-great-grandfather's business also cites an August 1839 newspaper article about a ride on the canal boat.

Excursion on the Canal
Messrs. Editors—
As one of a company which recently sailed up the canal to Broad Ripple, permit me to give you a short account of the voyage and its incidents, scenery, etc.
We left the lock at 8 A.M. being about thirty in number, and soon passed Cottonville, the sea[t] of the enterprising Mr. West. Here is one of the most delightful residences near the city, and highly improved; also one of the best mills (grist) and also a cotton spinning establishment in full and beautiful condition ...
... Having passed the [Fall Creek] aqueduct the country is more elevated and the soil is of a better quality, and I am told there is some of the finest tillable land on either side of the canal. The bluffs here on the right of the canal are high and remarkable, and furnish some of the most delightful sites for country residences to be imagined.[25] The breeze on the canal is very comfortable and refreshing. Three miles from town we passed McIlvain's bridge. Here the ground is a little rolling and beautiful. Shortly after this we passed near White

9

River, and the prospect here is delightful, there is a view of the river for half a mile, and the banks are beautifully adorned with shrubbery and flowers. The country here is delightful and productive.

We soon reached Broad Ripple, which is caused by a dam thrown across White River a little below the mouth of the canal to turn the water into it. The view here is beautiful. Here there is a most comfortable public house, kept by Mr. Earl, the enterprising and attentive owner of the boat. Here a number of the company spent the day delightfully, and partook of a good dinner and some fresh fish, others of the company amused themselves rambling on the banks of the river. In the evening we returned pleasantly and safely.

The late-nineteenth-century remembrances of one Franklin, Indiana, man suggest that the lock mentioned in the newspaper article, a stone structure at Market and Missouri streets, was the only canal lock actually completed. Two temporary wooden locks were built along the bluffs just below Kansas Street, but the locks' gates were never finished. The first three bridges across the canal were said to be at Michigan Road, Washington Street, and Kentucky Avenue; a fourth, built later, spanned the mill race at Market Street. The same memoir indicates that the canal also provided recreational facilities for some of the people living nearby. When water dammed up below a partially completed aqueduct over Pleasant Run, the site became a favorite fishing ground. A mile farther down the canal was a race track for "country quarter nags." And for several years, a break in the canal bank at Ray Street filled up a wooded area from Merrill to Morris streets, and children played in the ponds.[26]

Water power boosts business development

The water power generated by the canal played an important role in the development of several Indianapolis businesses, as one early twentieth-century history of the Indianapolis Water Company indicates:

In the years 1839-40, the state made contracts covering periods of thirty years for the power at the various places along the canal. The power at Broad Ripple was leased January 1, 1840, to [canal contractor] John Burke and [canal engineer] T. A. Morris at an annual rental of $250.00 and provided for the development of a power equal to two runs of 4-1/2 ft. mill stones. The second power was developed a short distance below Fall Creek south of the present location of the Indianapolis Water Company's [White River] filter plant and provided for power equal to two and a half runs of 4-1/2 ft. mill stones at a rental of $500.00 per year. The power site at the South Half of Block 50 in the City of Indianapolis [north of Market Street, between Missouri and West streets] was leased to Yandes & Sheets and was used in the development of a paper mill. The lease provided for the use of power, developed on a "pitch-back" wheel, ranging from three to four runs of 4-1/2 ft. mill stones at $150.00 per run per year. At the north end of the upper basin mentioned above, the power was leased to Wm. Sheets for two runs of 4-1/2 ft. mill stones at $300.00. At the south end of the lower basin, power was leased to Samuel and Jonathan Ogden to drive the saws for sawing timber at $600.00 per year. At the south end of the upper basin, the lease was made to C. T. Chamberlain for two runs of 4-1/2 ft. mill stones at $400.00. In Out Lot 145 [south of Washington Street, between Blackford and the river], the lease for the power was made to Merritt & Coughlen and was used in developing a woolen mill.

The annual rentals from these various [water power] leases constituted the only source of revenue for the state [and subsequent owners] from the Indianapolis Division of the Central Canal from 1840 to 1880,[27] and it was necessary for the state to keep quite a force working on the canal all the time in order to maintain the waterway in condition to provide the power which had been contracted for.

J. Darrell Bakken

Indiana sells the canal to out-of-state interests

The various pieces of public improvement work which had been started in 1837 by the state had gradually been taken over by private enterprises, most of the railroads which were comprised in the original 1300 miles as planned in 1836 being developed by individual companies during the decade ending 1850. The private companies did not seem anxious, however, to take over from the state the various pieces of canals which had been left in an unfinished condition, but in the year 1850 the State Legislature authorized the sale of so much of the Central Canal as had been built, it being divided into two parts for that purpose; that part south of the north line of Morgan County being sold in one block and all north of the north line of Morgan County in another. By a deed of June 30, 1851, the State of Indiana, by Joseph A. Wright, Governor, Charles H. Test, Secretary, and Erastus W. H. Ellis, Auditor of State, sold "All the right, title and interest of the State of Indiana in and to that portion of the Northern Division of the Central Canal situate North of Morgan County, including its banks, margins, tow-paths, side-cuts, feeders, basins, right-of-way, dams, water power, etc.," the grantee being Francis A. Conwell, who was the assignee of the three men who made the successful bid for the canal when it was sold at auction November 16th, 1850.[28]

The state's sale of the remaining Northern Division of the Central Canal to Conwell and other Rochester, New York, businessmen officially ended Indiana's financial losses on the project and foreshadowed the end of the state's canal fever. Indianapolis was by this time the third largest city in Indiana, after New Albany and Madison, with a population of about 8,000. It was to grow even larger in the years ahead, especially after the end of the Civil War. Despite the sale of the canal to out-of-state interests, the role it played in the development of the city was by no means over.

CHAPTER 2
PRIVATE OWNERS FAIL TO MAKE THE CANAL PROFITABLE

During the 1850s and 1860s the canal was in the hands of private owners. On June 30, 1851, the state of Indiana sold the canal to the Central Canal Manufacturing, Hydraulic, and Water Works Company of Rochester, New York. According to the deed abstract, the state sold "all the right, title and interest" to the Northern Division of the Central Canal (everything located north of the Johnson—Morgan county line at Waverly) to one Francis A. Conwell.[29] However, an act of the state General Assembly, approved February 13 of the same year, indicates that the canal was not sold to Conwell but to east-central Indiana businessmen George Shoup, James Rariden, and John S. Newman. The act authorized these three men to transfer title of the canal to the Central Canal Manufacturing, Hydraulic, and Water Works Company, composed of Francis Conwell, Henry Van Bergess, William Burnet, Luther Bingham, and David Worcester, and incorporated in Rochester, New York.[30]

Thomas A. Morris, Central Canal engineer, and Alexander Morrison, acting canal commissioner in 1838, were appointed by the general assembly in 1850 to set the selling price of the canal. They set the valuation at $2,425, a small sum compared with the reported construction cost of $435,496.[31] According to Morris's memoirs of the canal, it "was sold to parties in New York."[32]

Published histories give various facts and sequences of events about the canal's ownership during this period. The correct sequence appears to be:

1. Indiana's General Assembly on January 21, 1850, authorized the governor, secretary of state, and state auditor to sell the Northern Division of the Central Canal.

2. The General Assembly appointed former canal

13

engineer Thomas A. Morris and former acting canal commissioner Alexander Morrison to value the canal and authorized its sale at their valuation of $2,425.

3. The canal was sold without deed in 1850 to Shoup, Rariden, and Newman of eastern Indiana—investors also involved in Indiana's Whitewater Canal—for $2,425.

4. For an unknown price, Shoup, Rariden, and Newman assigned the canal purchase to Francis Conwell and four other members of the Central Canal Manufacturing, Hydraulic, and Water Works Company (CCMH & WWC) of Rochester, New York, in accord with the General Assembly's act of February 13, 1851.

5. A deed dated June 30, 1851, was executed, conveying the canal's title to Francis Conwell.

6. The second and third entries in the 1881 deed abstract conveyed title from individuals in Rochester, New York, to the CCMH & WWC. Francis A. Conwell and his wife Mary M. Conwell executed a warranty deed to Marcus T. C. Gould and Jeremiah Jackson. Gould and Jackson and their wives (Maria Gould and Mary L. Jackson) deeded the canal to the company.

Maintenance costs exceed the canal's income from water power

Jeremiah Jackson, though not listed as one of the principals in the February 1851 legislation, appears to be a major player in the canal's history, according to an Indianapolis *Journal* article of November 15, 1851:

We understand that Dr. Ramsay, Agent for the Company, F. C. Moore, Engineer, and Mr. Jeremiah Jackson, one of the principal Stockholders in the Central Canal Company, passed over the entire line of the Canal, from this city [north] to where it strikes the Wabash and Erie Canal, for the purpose of examining whether it was practicable for the company to go on and finish the canal to connect with the Wabash and Erie Canal. Of course the result and determination cannot be known until Mr. Jackson reports to the stockholders in New York, but from the very favorable opinion he has formed of the country through which the canal passes, and the comparatively small amount necessary to complete it, we have no doubt but the company will commence next spring, and push it through as fast as the work can be done. Should they determine to undertake the work, of which we have little doubt, they will most probably have it finished to Anderson next year, and form the connection of the northern water communication [from Anderson to the Wabash and Erie Canal and on] to New York by the year following.[33]

There is no indication that any additional construction on the Central Canal ever took place toward Anderson or toward the Wabash and Erie Canal from Anderson. Contemporary histories suggest instead that the Central Canal Company of the 1850s, like the state of Indiana in the 1840s, was unsuccessful in completing the Central Canal or in making it a profitable venture, primarily because of high annual maintenance costs. The cost of keeping the canal full of water for power to be used by the mills along its banks considerably exceeded annual income from water power.

In 1857, by a quit-claim deed, ownership of the canal changed hands again. In April 1857 the Indianapolis *Journal* reported that:

We hear that [Indianapolis] Judge William McCarty has bought the Central Canal. It is to be hoped that he will use it not only to his own advantage, but to that of the city. With an expenditure of a comparatively small sum of money, an amount of water can be brought down the canal which will afford ample power for manufacturing purposes. Indianapolis needs all the manufacturing facilities that can be afforded... .[34]

Indeed, by this time water from the canal may have been

powering as many as fourteen mills in Indianapolis and Broad Ripple—including sawmills, gristmills, paper mills, oil mills, and cotton mills. Annual lease payments for water power from all of these manufacturers, however, totaled less than $10,000.[35]

In 1857 and again in 1858 the Indianapolis city council threatened to interfere with the use of the canal for industrial power by asserting its right to issue permits to a railroad (to build a bridge across the canal) and to local contractors (to fill in canal crossings for road construction). Judge McCarty, holder of the quitclaim deed for the canal, issued a reply to the council in an Indianapolis newspaper, stating that (1) the owner of the canal was granted all rights to it directly from the state and (2) the city had no rights to the canal except those granted in writing by the canal's owner.[36]

Like the state and private owners before him, however, the judge soon tired of the financial losses associated with owning the canal as well as the squabbles with the city and its residents. On January 9, 1859, he conveyed a quitclaim deed for the canal back to Nicholas Paine of Rochester, New York. A series of ten quitclaim deeds from January 1859 until April 18, 1863 (including a February 5, 1859, deed to Calvin T. Chamberlain of Rochester) resulted in transfer of the title to the Indiana Central Canal Company of Rochester, New York.[37]

Despite the numerous changes in canal ownership, the Indianapolis *Journal* continued to proclaim confidence in proposed improvements to the canal and in the potential for these improvements to facilitate community expansion. In March 1859 the following article appeared:

The canal has passed into the possession of E. [Calvin] T. Chamberlain and others, wealthy gentlemen of Rochester, New York, who have expended some $10,000 in the liquidation of taxes and other claims.... . The public work is now in hands which will make it valuable to the city—benefiting its owners directly and the public indirectly.... . the canal may now be regarded as a permanent

16

"institution" capable of increasing our manufacturing facilities more than a hundred fold. The power that will be afforded after all the contemplated improvements are made will be sufficient to drive eighty or ninety ton of stones at all seasons of the year. Men of observation and judgment pronounce it one of the best hydraulic works in the Union. There is a mine of wealth in the productive industry which the Canal is destined to unfold.

The December 2, 1859, *Journal* recorded that the New York canal owners had spent $20,000 (rather than $10,000 as reported in March) to quiet all claims against the Central Canal. The newspaper also reported that the owners had assisted two or three additional manufacturers who would use canal water power in starting their businesses.[38]

Proposals suggest using the canal for public water supply

A new use of canal water—for public water supply by a new water utility—was suggested in the Canal Company's 1859 official report, published in the Indianapolis *Journal* in February 1860.[39] This report, the first of seven proposals the city would receive regarding formation of a water utility, was written by engineer Daniel Marsh, of Rochester, New York, who had been engaged by the Canal Company the previous year. The report was forwarded to the city council and referred to a select committee, which requested that it be published in city newspapers.

In his report, Marsh recommended a new water supply of 1 million gallons per day for an 1860 population of 18,611—54 gallons per person per day. He proposed that water be taken from the canal 4 miles above the city,[40] pumped by two overshot water wheels to a reservoir of "two or three acres of water surface and fifteen feet in depth" on Crown Hill, and conveyed by gravity to the central city through a 14-inch main. Marsh estimated that this supply system and 150,000 feet (28 miles) of distribution mains would cost $146,000 if wooden mains were used or $255,000 if cast-iron mains were chosen. According to Jacob Dunn's history of Indianapolis, the income expected to accrue from this proposed utility was estimated at $31,515: $7,000 from the city, $4,800 from railroads, $3,000 from the state, and $16,715 from water customers. [41]

Publication of the Marsh report prompted a second water utility proposal, published in a local newspaper, from Ryland T. Brown. Brown claimed that there were three possibilities for city water supply—cisterns, an aqueduct, and artesian or flowing wells. He also claimed that the first two options would not supply either pure or cold water. A deep artesian well, by Brown's estimates, would cost about $3,000, and he predicted that the water would be brackish and taste like sulfur. A more shallow artesian well, however, drilled through the hardpan clay to water-bearing sand would cost only $150 to $200 and, according to Brown, would give good, cool water that might rise to the surface or even higher. The newspaper article also reported that, after discussion by the city council, drilling for a shallow artesian well at the local insane asylum had been started, but the proposed well had been abandoned when drillers struck a boulder at 72 feet. The city council took no further action on either the Marsh or Brown proposals. [42]

On July 15, 1864, the Central Canal Company approached the city again, proposing to organize a private water company and to furnish the rapidly growing city with water from the canal. This proposal received only slight consideration. A fourth proposal was considered in August 1864, when Mayor John Caven revived Brown's proposal for an artesian well and apparently also suggested Crown Hill as a site for a reservoir. [43] The only decision the city council made regarding these 1864 proposals was that the city should not design, construct, or operate a water utility but should instead grant a long-term franchise or charter to a private company. In 1866 one such company came forward.

On November 3, 1866, the city council granted a charter to R. B. Catherwood and Company for a water supply company known as the Indianapolis Water Company. This was the city's fifth proposal concerning the formation of a water utility. According to the requirements of the charter (1) the water supply would be taken from the White River several miles above the city, (2) the company would spend a certain amount of money on the water system within a specified time period, (3) fire hydrants—purchased at a set price to be paid annually by the city—would be located where the city ordered, and (4) the city would have the option to purchase the utility after twenty-five years. The company was organized with R. B. Catherwood as president and John S. Tarkington as secretary. It installed about 50 feet of water mains in North Street within one year, but it did nothing after 1867, and its charter was revoked November 30, 1868. [44]

In August of 1868 the Indianapolis Fire Department obtained a city council appropriation of $600 to drill a well for fire protection at the corner of University Square and Vermont Street. By September 14 the department's chief engineer reported that $944 had been spent, the well was 66½ feet deep, and the project was as yet unsuccessful. Although another appropriation allowed the depth of the well to be extended to 92 feet, the driller then "quit and left the city, leaving the sand pump fast in the bottom of the well." The well and the project were soon abandoned, but the importance of fire protection water service for the city would again be raised in 1870, when the council authorized the first actual water utility. [45]

Late that same summer, the Central Canal Company of Rochester, New York, renewed its 1864 proposal to develop a water supply from the canal. The proposal, which specified a Holly steam pumping system and cast-iron water mains to provide ample water at sufficient pressures for domestic use and fire protection, included selling the Central Canal to the city for $200,000. [46] In January of 1869 engineer William C. Weir reported to the city council that the canal water supply, the pumping system, and the mains would cost an additional $350,000. Weir recommended taking water from the canal at the Broad Cut basin (now located adjacent to the White River Purification Plant at about West 20th Street), where turbidity could settle out. Canal water would be conveyed via approximately 9,000 feet of wooden conduit to a Holly pump station on the east bank of the White River at Washington Street, a site that became the location of the first Washington Station pump house in 1871. Weir also proposed about 35 miles of cast-iron water mains of 4 to 16 inches in diameter. Like others before it, however, this proposal came to an unsuccessful end—and this time for the most mundane of reasons:

A committee was appointed by the mayor to visit some city where Water Works were already in operation under the Holly system, but as the Council required the members of the committee to pay their own expenses on the trip, the matter was dropped. [47] As indicated earlier, the council in 1865 had expressed the intent that the city would not design, construct, own, or operate a water utility, and its subsequent decisions confirmed this accord.

The seventh, finally successful, proposal to create a water utility for the city of Indianapolis was officially initiated on October 7, 1869, by James O. Woodruff (who had moved to the city from Rochester, New York) and eight prominent local business and professional men.

This proposal included a new use for canal water in addition to transportation and water power for mills—high-lift pumping of treated water into the distribution system using turbines powered by canal water.

Legal ownership of the Central Canal thus returned from New York to Indiana in 1869—1870 for the second time since the canal's sale by the state in 1851. After twenty years of operating losses by two companies, a number of failed plans to increase water-use income from various sources, and six attempts to form a water utility for the city, control of the Central Canal was back home in Indiana.

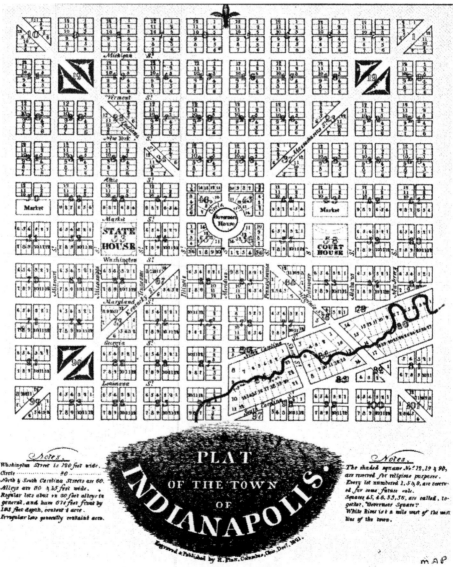

1821 engraving of the original plan for downtown Indianapolis
Courtesy Indiana State Library

INDIANA.

We learn, from New York, that on the 8th instant, the Fund Commissioners of Indiana sold one million of her 5 per cent. bonds at 2 per cent. premium. This with $300,000 sold a few days before at par, and $400,000, for which the Commissioners received in cash $8000—for the option at the end of sixty days to take it at par, makes $1,700,000, which this rising state finds herself able to raise, at an interest of less than 5 per cent. to enable her to carry on her bold and comprehensive system of Internal Improvements. This result is most flattering to our sister State, and we rejoice with her at the evidence it affords of her high credit. When Ohio commenced her canals in 1825, she was only able to sell her 5 per cent. for $97 50 per share, while Indiana is in these times able to realize $102 upon the same description of stock. Why then should any portion of the people of Indiana be disheartened with her undertaking. It is true she has, perhaps, undertaken too much at one time; but having put her hand to the plough and having began the system under such favorable auspices, she cannot, with justice or credit to herself, turn back. Every thing is favorable to the cheap and speedy consummation of the gigantic schemes of Internal improvement, which our sister state has adopted. Money is at her command—laborers are abundant —and both labor and provisions are cheap. "Go ahead!" then should be the motto of every genuine Indianian.—Cin. Repub.

Newspaper report of canal funding
Courtesy IHS

INDIANAPOLIS:

Tuesday, Jan. 19, 1836.

INTERNAL IMPROVEMENT BILL
PASSED.

The important, and, for the last few days, all-absorbing bill providing for a general system of internal improvements has received, in its important features, the sanction of both Houses of the General Assembly. It passed the Senate about 2 o'clock on Saturday, after a very laborious morning's session. The Senate made but few amendments, and they not very essential. It is not apprehended that they will produce any diff----

The road-bed to be graded for a double track.

Also at Indianapolis, on the 4th day of October next, by D. Burr, Acting Commissioner, for the construction of 25 miles of the Central Canal, extending from the feeder dam above Indianapolis to "the Bluffs." This line embraces a Dam across the White river, an Adqueduct over Fall creek, 8 Lift Locks, most of which will be built of cut stone, 2 or 3 Bluff sections, and several large Culverts.

Newspaper notice of the Internal Improvements Act

23

Surveying for the new capital, 1820, painting by Thomas B. Glessing

Courtesy Indiana State Library

Construction on the Wabash and Erie Canal, painting by Wils Burry

Courtesy Tippecanoe County Historical Society

2,000 LABORERS WANTED ON THE CENTRAL CANAL Of Indiana.

THE great Central Canal of Indiana is intended to connect the waters of Lake Erie and the Ohio river, and will be about 400 miles in length. In addition to that part already completed and under contract in the middle and northern part of the state, TWENTY miles commencing at Evansville, on the Ohio river, its southern termination, and extending into the interior, were put under contract in November last; since which time the work has been steadily progressing.

No section of country holds out greater inducements to the industrious laborer than the state of Indiana, and particularly that portion of it contiguous to the Central Canal, from the fact that there is much of the land belonging to the general government remaining unentered, which may be purchased at one dollar and twenty-five cents per acre; affording to those who are desirous of doing so, an opportunity of securing to themselves, with the avails of a few months' labor, a permanent home in this flourishing and rapidly growing state.

The contractors are now paying $20 per month, and the fare and lodgings furnished, is of the most comfortable character. It may not be amiss to say that the acting commissioner reserves, by an express provision in all contracts, the right to see that every laborer receives his just dues; therefore, no man need lose one dollar of his wages, if he pursues a proper course.

It is probable that more of this Canal will be put under contract during the coming fall or spring, when an opportunity will be offered to those who show themselves qualified of proposing for work.

Laborers coming from the south can take passage to Evansville, and find immediate employment upon their arrival. By order of JOHN A. GRAHAM, *Act. Com.*
Canal Office, Evansville, May 1, 1837. C. G. VOORHIES, *Res'dt Eng.*

EVANSVILLE JOURNAL Printers.

1837 broadside seeking laborers for the canal

Courtesy Indiana State Library

J. Darrell Bakken

Beginning of the canal at Broad Ripple dam

Courtesy IWC

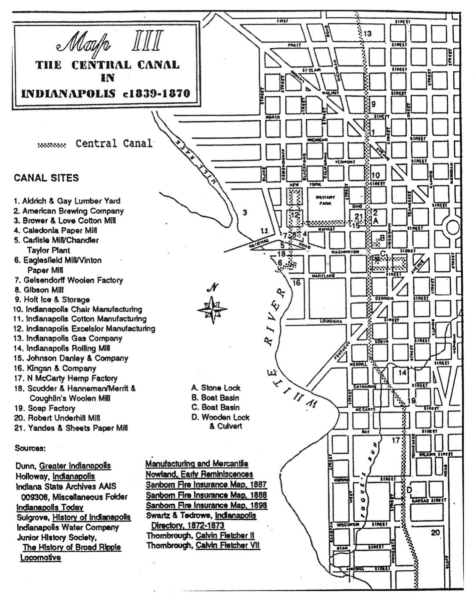

Map of canal waters users

Courtesy Rita W. Harlan

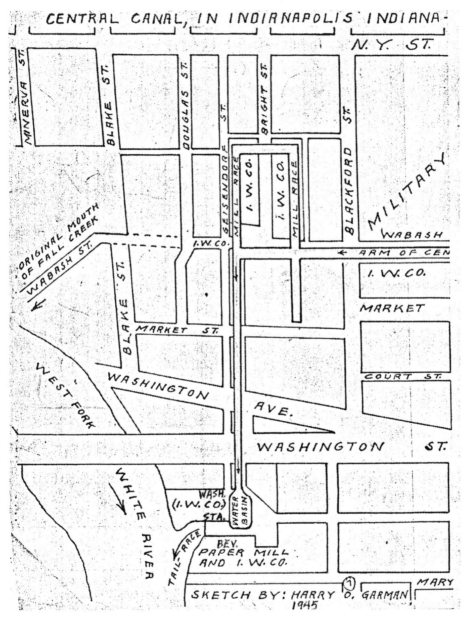

Canal in downtown Indianapolis

Courtesy IWC

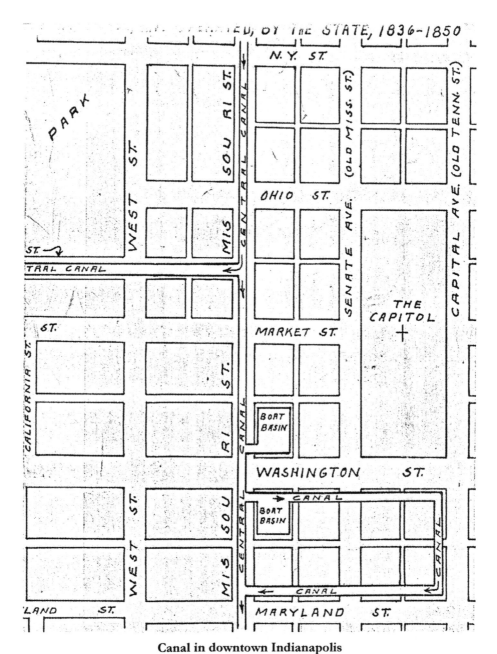

Canal in downtown Indianapolis

Courtesy Indiana State Library

A canal lock at Sheets Paper Mill on Market Street, sketch by Christian Schrader

Schrader sketch of Washington Street bridge and canal boat

Courtesy Indiana State Library

Schrader sketch of the original Washington Street bridge over the canal

Schrader sketch of early mills in Indianapolis

Courtesy Indiana State Library

CHAPTER 3
CANAL WATER POWERS TURBINES TO PUMP DRINKING WATER

By 1870 the population of Indianapolis had reached more than 48,000, but the city did not yet have a public water supply. The canal was still being used for only two purposes: water-wheel power and transportation of freight and passengers. By this time, many of the original mills that held thirty-year contracts for water power from the canal had gone out of business, and transportation contracts were intermittent or short-lived. The third primary owner of the canal, the Indiana Central Canal Company, was able to renew only a few of the original thirty-year power contracts, and the owners who followed immediately after experienced similar bad fortune.

The Water Works Company of Indianapolis takes over the canal

The next company to own the Central Canal (the third private company and the first based in Indianapolis) was the Water Works Company of Indianapolis (WWCI), officially formed October 7, 1869. [48] WWCI's first president, James O. Woodruff, was a New Yorker from Rochester; the remainder of the incorporators were Hoosiers Dr. William Braden, George Stilz, W. M. Wiles, J. A. Comingore, George F. McGinnis, Thomas A. Hendricks, James E. Mooney, and Albert G. Porter. [49]

The WWCI received its first franchise through a city council ordinance November 15, 1869. [50] In January of the next year, this document was replaced by one more favorable to the company. [51] Both ordinances are discussed here because they contain numerous city council requirements regarding water supply, water purity, pumping pressure, and fire flows and because they remained Indianapolis's public water utility franchise documents until 1923. [52]

The Indiana Central Canal Company of Rochester, New York, conveyed the warranty deed for the Central Canal to WWCI on May 1, 1870, and the deed was recorded December 28, 1870. WWCI was reportedly organized with $500,000 of capital stock. [53]

Canal powers turbines to pump water for domestic use and fire protection

The January 1870 ordinance required WWCI to begin development of a water utility within three months; to construct—within another fifteen months at considerable cost—a water well supply, a pump house, and a dual pumping system for domestic water use and fire protection; and to install at least 5 miles of cast-iron water mains. The company was required to connect 10 additional miles of mains to the water system within another year.

The council's requirement for a new pumping system gave WWCI an opportunity to use the canal's water in two new ways: to power turbines for pumping into the water mains and to provide high-pressure public fire protection. No ordinances, however, required city residents along the system of mains to give up their private wells and become WWCI customers. This lack of incentive would prove fatal to the new company, particularly in light of the high costs incurred during its first years of business. Two studies indicate that WWCI paid $200,000 for the Central Canal. [54] According to the company's first annual report in 1871, expenditures for real estate, liens, and "sundry pieces of ground" totaled $522,668. [55]

In May 1871 WWCI posted notice in the Indianapolis *Journal* that a public water works utility was ready for continuous 24-hour service from its new Washington Station at Washington Street and the east bank of the White River. The company claimed to have one large-diameter well, a 6-million-gallon-per-day Holly pump powered by a steam engine, three high-service pumps driven by canal water power, a large pump house, 5 miles of water mains, and 200 fire hydrants. An adjacent article reported that WWCI had spent $400,000 to $500,000 on the water system to date. [56] By autumn a second large-diameter well was in service, at the request of the city, and 20 miles of water mains had been installed by the end of the year. [57] The company retained John N. Hurty, chief chemist for local pharmaceutical manufacturer Johnstone and Lilly, to perform its water quality analyses. [58]

By January 1, 1873, WWCI had acquired only 784 customers. In a city of 50,000, the company could conceivably have been serving 10,000 households as well as businesses and government buildings. [59] Despite this lack of success, work continued. WWCI constructed another 6-million-gallon Holly pump in 1874, added a filter crib in and under White River in 1875 to expand the water supply, installed 10 more miles of water mains that same year and another 10 miles in 1876, and added 365 more fire hydrants. Much of this expansion occurred in response to two events of the spring of 1874.

In late March the Sheets Hotel Fire, "the most disastrous the city had yet had," caused $300,000 worth of damage. A special city council waterworks committee quickly met to assess possible solutions. The committee's report ignored the potential culpability of the city's fire department and recommended instead that the city build a second waterworks of its own at an estimated cost of $1 million. The new, separate fire protection system would have consisted of a 30-million-gallon reservoir on Crown Hill, a dam on White River to the west of Crown Hill with a pump to bring river water to the new reservoir, a 2-mile-long water transmission line from Crown Hill to about Tinker Street (now 16th Street), and a series of water mains and hydrants (in addition to those already built by WWCI) from West Street to East Street and from Tinker Street on the north to Morris Street on the south. In the May 5 city election, however, voters soundly defeated the proposal: 2,142 for and 6,800 against. [60]

Operations, Maintenance, and Legal Problems for WWCI

WWCI experienced a decade of operation and maintenance

problems with the Central Canal. The first problems involved the Market Street mill race arm from Market and Missouri to the east bank of White River south of Washington Street. The company had added the Washington Station pump house and its canal-powered pumps to the mills already using water power from that arm of the canal. Several of these mills were operating under long-term contracts—their initial thirty-year contracts extending to 1869 or 1870 had been renewed for another thirty years just before the canal deed was transferred to the WWCI. Several lawsuits charging WWCI with inadequate and intermittent service of water power were pending. In the spring of 1873 all of the company's stockholders were indicted in Marion County criminal court for maintaining a nuisance in the Market Street mill race arm. The company claimed that the problems were caused by the city, which allowed street drainage to flow into the canal without rights or permission and which permitted adjacent property owners to empty sinks, drains, and filth into the canal. The case was dismissed when WWCI promised to clean up the mill race arm. [61]

A more serious problem occurred along the primary canal route along Missouri Street south of the Market Street mill race. The remainder of the working canal at that time ran generally southward to Pleasant Run, the practical terminus of the canal when construction ceased in 1839. Originally, no users of canal water had been located along Missouri Street from Market to Merrill Streets. But there had been four water-power contracts with mills along the canal south of Merrill Street—the Rolling Mill at Merrill and Tennessee, a soap factory at McCarty and Tennessee, a hemp factory at Ray and Tennessee, and the Robert Underhill Grist Mill at Wisconsin and Bluff. By 1870 only the Rolling Mill remained. [62]

While the state and two private companies attempted to maintain water power for the mills from 1839 to 1870, residents on both sides of the canal used the water as an open sewer for easy dumping of trash and other wastes. After two years of pressure from the public, the city council, and the press, WWCI deeded most of the real estate involved with the Central Canal (from Market Street to Merrill or Morris Street) to the Indianapolis, Cincinnati and Lafayette Railroad Company, as indicated by an 1873 deed, and abandoned the rest. [63]

An 1872 lawsuit was also costly to WWCI. By that year five ice companies were harvesting block ice from the Central Canal, and WWCI was sued over who had legal rights to the ice. The utility apparently won the lawsuit because they, and IWC in 1910, continued to license use of the canal by ice companies. [64]

First Re-Survey of Canal Land and the End of the WWCI

In 1877 Joseph H. Dennis, deputy Marion County surveyor, performed the first complete re-survey of the remaining canal. The last major survey had taken place in the 1830s, when Thomas A. Morris surveyed the route for the canal's initial construction. [65] Some forty years later, only one-third of the original 25-mile Central Canal remained in service.

By 1880 the end of WWCI was near. The city of Indianapolis had grown to just over 75,000 people, with an estimated 15,000 households. WWCI had installed 47 miles of water mains and 601 hydrants, but claimed only 1,400 customers. No longer able to make interest payments on the bonds sold to pay for the improvements of 1874 to 1876, the company went into receivership. On April 21, 1881, the Marion county sheriff sold WWCI to the Indianapolis Water Company for $500,000. The sheriff's deed of that date lists WWCI's debts at $1,130,156, an amount incurred after only ten years of operation. [66]

WWCI had returned ownership of the canal to Indianapolis, and the company could claim one major accomplishment during its decade of owning and operating the canal: initiating a significant new use for canal water, i.e., powering turbines to pump drinking water into the distribution system. [67]

CHAPTER 4
THE CANAL BECOMES A FINANCIAL ASSET

A newly formed, locally owned Indianapolis Water Company (IWC) purchased the assets of the bankrupt WWCI at a sheriff's sale on the county courthouse steps on April 21, 1881. IWC became the canal's fifth owner. The sale also gave the company $1.5 million worth of wells, high-lift pumps, water mains, and fire hydrants, but only 1,400 customers. [68]

Indianapolis Water Company expands its customer base

The new IWC officers and board must have recognized that if their company was to become viable, they needed to convince a substantial percentage of the potential residential customers, as well as many businesses and industries, to abandon their shallow, private wells and connect to company water mains. Most water power contracts signed by the state and privately owned mills had expired years earlier, many before WWCI took over ownership of the canal. But even if all of these contracts had still been in place, total water-wheel revenue would have been no more than $15,000 per year, less than the $25,000 annual interest on the bonds that financed IWC's $500,000 purchase. [69] Revenues from canal freight and excursion boats were also low, as they had been from the canal's beginnings in 1839. [70]

In addition, the company needed water treatment processes that could transform its most economical raw water supply, the White River, into safe, potable water for the city.

The first IWC officers were T. Edward Hambleton (president), Sidney W. Dyer (vice-president), F. A. W. Davis (treasurer), and John H. Langdon (secretary). [71] The company also had a board of directors, consisting of the four officers and nine other members, many prominent community leaders. [72] In late 1881 General Thomas A. Morris took over as president of the company. [73]

At its May 28, 1881, meeting, the board authorized up to $150,000 to be spent to increase the company's supply of pure water. J. James R. Croes, a New York waterworks engineer, was hired to head the search for the new water supply, and John N. Hurty was retained to conduct chemical and other sanitary analyses. [74] The two consultants recommended an infiltration gallery, or horizontal well, 1,500 feet long, 50 feet wide, and 35 feet deep to be built on farmland northwest of downtown. Their recommendation echoed that of local pharmaceutical manufacturer Eli Lilly, who had already written letters to the editor of the Indianapolis *News* in August 1881. By 1883 the gallery had been constructed north of relocated Fall Creek (and what is now West 10th Street) on the east side of the White River. [75] Groundwater was conveyed south from the infiltration gallery to Washington Station by a 30-inch-diameter gravity concrete conduit more than 7,000 feet long. About one fifth of the conduit was laid in the abandoned bed of Fall Creek. In the same year the company also added a pair of Holly rotary pumps at Washington Station to increase its system's pumping capacity to 22 mgd.

The flood of 1883 washed out part of the gallery next to White River, taking it out of service. The water company erected a wall across the end of the remaining gallery, built a wing dam out into the river to protect the revised gallery, and constructed a covered gallery that was connected to the existing open gallery by a tunnel. The covered gallery also served as a filter crib, similar to the one WWCI had constructed adjacent to Washington Station in the late 1870s, to supplement the supply from its two large-diameter wells. According to a 1908 history of IWC, the gallery water supply was fed by a spring essentially uncontaminated by any surrounding development. [76]

By 1891 IWC had doubled the number of customers it began with; by 1898 that 2,800 had increased to 8,000; and by the end of 1904, according to a consultant's report, there were 14,296 city water customers. The number of potential customers was also expanding. In 1890 the city's population surpassed 105,000, and by 1904 the potential customer base had almost doubled to 197,000. [77] The rapid growth brought the need for a new water supply as well as more pumping stations and water mains.

In 1889 IWC added two more high-lift pumps at Washington Station. From 1889 to 1892 the company purchased sixty-seven more acres of land north of Fall Creek, constructed a second Holly—Gaskill pump station (located behind what is now Riverside Station), and drilled wells at the new location. By 1896 IWC owned 250 acres of land surrounding the Riverside complex. The company had drilled twenty-six deep wells into the underlying limestone formations and was producing 12 to 14 mgd. In 1898 the company added the Snow Pump Station at Riverside.

Even with this capacity, IWC needed to develop an additional supply because of the rapidly increasing population and the growing number of water system connections. In 1896 the company hired two well-respected consultants, Allen Hazen and E. G. Smith, to find and design this new supply. Hazen and Smith recommended a surface water treatment plant that would utilize the huge raw water supply of the White River available via the Central Canal. The plant was to be built at the canal's broadcut at about West 20th Street, extending between Fall Creek on the west and the canal on the east. [78] Six slow-sand filter units, with a total treated water capacity of 36 mgd, were constructed from 1904 through 1905. [79] Sixty-five years after the canal's completion, IWC had finally transformed it into a financial asset and a major part of the water supply system for Indianapolis.

The IWC took other actions to ensure future utility expansion. In 1898 the company purchased Schofield Mill and Dam on Fall Creek for water rights on a future surface water supply. A third pumping unit at Riverside, the Davis pump, was completed from 1901 to 1904. In 1902 the company engaged consulting engineer Joseph H. Dennis, who had conducted the 1877 canal survey, to study the feasibility of an off-stream storage reservoir on a low tract of land west of the canal (a site that now comprises the lake and gardens of the Indianapolis Museum of Art). [80] Morris and his officers and board also actively developed the IWC in other ways. In 1891 the company purchased a headquarters site in the heart of the city on Monument Circle. From 1881 through 1909 the officers also directed community development projects that resulted in major recreational uses of the canal.

Citizens use the canal and adjacent city parks for recreation

The Central Canal had often been used for recreation since its inception in 1839, when horses pulled excursion boats of sightseers along its channel. After 1881 IWC cleaned up the canal's right-of-way and greatly improved overall maintenance, thus increasing the waterway's potential for recreational uses. Contemporary sources in the 1880s and 1890s mention people walking along the canal towpath, young couples canoeing from the rental building at Fairview Park to the canal aqueduct over Fall Creek, and families ice skating in the winter. The canal's banks also afforded sites for cycling, picnicking, and, of course, fishing.

Parks along the canal enhanced its recreational uses. Access to the canal was available from Fairview Park (now Holcomb Gardens at Butler University) in the 1890s through the early 1920s, Armstrong Park (32nd to 34th Streets on the east side of the canal) in the 1880s and 1890s, and Riverside Amusement Park (West 30th Street) from 1902 until its closing in 1970. The IWC had its own steamboats, the *Diane* and the *Cleopatra*, which offered rides on the canal, and independent businessman Otto Schissel offered swimming lessons at a bathhouse built over the downtown mill race.

Fairview Park had been created in 1889 when the Citizens Street Railway Company purchased a 246-acre farm along the canal. The railway built a 12-mile streetcar line (the city's first electric line) from downtown to the park. A five-cent fare paid for the streetcar ride as well as admission to the park. The park included many concessions, including a water tank and tower for high-diving horses and a boathouse, located on the canal, where visitors could rent a canoe or take a ride on a steam-powered, flat-bottom boat. [81]

The east canal bank at Armstrong Park was apparently the

location of a boat dock. To this day, the piers of the dock still protrude from the water at about West 32nd Street. The dock served passengers who were en route to the Woodstock Club, including, in 1896, the wives of those attending the annual American Water Works Association national convention being held in Indianapolis. A more sensational entertainment at the park was a man who walked on the water of the canal using cleverly constructed galvanized footgear. [82]

Riverside Amusement Park began operation in 1902 along the east bank of the White River at 30th Street. The park offered an Old Mill ride, reported to be a replica of a working flour mill, which used canal water for a boat ride through a tunnel. [83]

In 1875 a bathhouse was built over the canal on the south side of Wabash Street just east of the West Street Bridge, and in the 1880s Otto Schissel's swimming school offered lessons at the site. Students were placed in harnesses attached to a long pole and then dipped into the water until they learned to swim. [84] In 1907 the Indianapolis *News* reported that William L. Taylor had purchased Schissel's bathhouse and donated it to the Children's Aid Society so that poor children could enjoy free swimming. The nation's vice-president, native Hoosier Charles Warren Fairbanks, presided over the bathhouse's rededication. [85]

By 1904 the IWC was supplying, on average, more than 16 million gallons of drinking water per day to 14,296 residential and business customers. The White River via the canal provided a plentiful supply of raw water, and increased demand for treated water in the future would require only additional treatment plants and associated infrastructure. For several decades to come, no major new water supplies would be necessary.

IWC became the first owner of the canal to recoup its investment, and it was the first owner to seriously develop long-term recreational uses for the canal. The company's commitment to maintenance and general care-taking created a community asset that has continued to the present day.

left unsold 60 lots. During this time quite a number of other large additions have been in the market. This shows two things, to-wit: First, the energy of the agents; second, the popularity of the addition. Those who may want lots in this deservedly popular addition had better call at once, for they will all be closed out in less than thirty days, as we are informed by said agent.

We have just been informed that Carlin Hamlin, some ten days since, purchased lot number 16 in Johnson's heirs' addition in that beautiful orchard just east of the Fair Grounds, and has subdivided the same into lots, and sold off two of the lots at $790 each, before he had time to stake off the ground—the only wonder is that he had time to drive the stakes, for it is certainly the most beautiful ground about the city. This ground is about 20 feet higher than Washington street, and all covered over with beautiful fruit trees, known as the best fruit about the city. There will be no trouble in selling these lots. These lots are for sale by Jacob T. Wright, No. 16 North Delaware street.

Over three million dollars worth of real estate has passed hands in this county since January 1st, 1871. Nearly or quite all of this has been in the city. The great bulk of it has been sold through the real estate office of Jacob T. Wright, and the great secret of his success is that he knows how to advertise—there is power in printer's ink.

INDIANAPOLIS AND ITS PUBLIC IMPROVEMENTS.—Our city now numbers over 50,000 souls, and is rapidly increasing in wealth and population. As an evidence of this we will mention but a few items: The Holly Water Works are being constructed at an outlay of between $400,000 and $500,000; new bridge across White river on Washington street, $70,000; new Court House, $600,000; new Hotel on North Pennsylvania street, $205,000. Besides this there are being expended tens of thousands of dollars in the construction of sewers, improvement of streets and the like. Jacob T. Wright, the real estate agent, informs us that almost every day parties call upon him from a distance, eastern capitalists and manufacturers, with a view of making profitable investments, and of establishing themselves at our beautiful healthy, and rapidly growing Hoosier Capitol.

IF YOU WANT MONEY

you can make it by taking an agency for the Bloss Noiseless, Link-motion, Lock-stitch Sewing Machine, the cheapest first class sewing machine made. Agents wanted in every city, county and town in the State. Address for terms, J. L. MANLOVE, General Agent, 65 East Market street, Indianapolis, Ind. apr26 3m

LAZARUS & MORRIS' perfected spectacles are the best; they never tire the eyes, last many years without change, are warranted not to break. C. A. Ferguson, jeweler and optician, No. 7 West Washington street, is sole agent for this city. may16 1m

ACADEMY OF MUSIC.

MACH BROS...........................Managers
Also of the Buffalo Academy of Music.

FOR TWO NIGHTS ONLY!

AND SATURDAY MATINEE.

Appearance of the famous young character Comedian,

MR. JOSEPH K. EMMET,

In his great specialty,

THE GERMAN EMIGRANT!

OR

FRIDAY AND SATURDAY EVENINGS.

AND SATURDAY MATINEE, JUNE 2d and 34.

In Chas. Gayler's successful Drama, in three acts, as performed for over Six Hundred Nights, including Wallack's Theater, New York, Seventy-five consecutive nights, called

FRITZ, OUR COUSIN GERMAN.

Fritz Von Vonderblinkenstoffer—Joseph K. Emmet, in which he will introduce his charming characteristic melange, Songs, Dances and Instrumental Solos, aided by a powerful Dramatic Company, with new scenery and appointments. For particulars see programmes.

ADMISSION.

Parquette and Dress Circle...............50 cents
Family Circle..............................35 cents
Gallery....................................25 cents
Reserved Seats.............................75 cents

Seats can be secured at Pearson & Dickson's Confectionary, under Academy of Music, on Wednesday morning, May 31. my29 6t

WATER SUPPLY.

WATER SUPPLY.

On and after THURSDAY, June 1, 1871, the machinery of the Water Works Company of Indianapolis, will be run day and night for supplying the city and citizens with water. From June 1st all consumers will be required to pay water rates.

Copies of the water rates proposed by the Company to the City Council for their approval, together with the rules and regulations governing the use of water, can be obtained at the office of the Company, No. 21 South Pennsylvania street.

JOHN R. ELDER, Vice-President.
ALEX. C. JAMESON, Secretary
Indianapolis, May 30, 1871—my31 3t

COPYING BOOKS, &c.

LETTER COPYING BOOKS,

LETTER PRESSES,

COPYING INKS,

With a full line of

OFFICE STATIONERY,

—AT—

BOWEN, STEWART & CO.'S.

last 6m-6thp

Indianapolis <u>Journal</u>, May 31, 1871, notice of new city water company

Original Washington Station (1871-1927)

Holly steam pump at Washington Station

Courtesy IWC

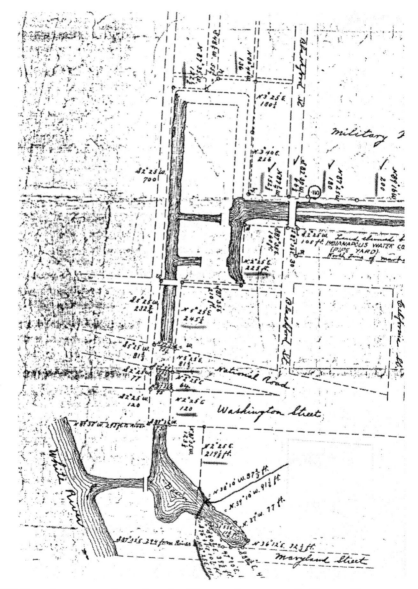

1877 Dennis survey of canal and mill race, downtown Indianapolis

Courtesy IWC

877 Dennis survey of canal and mill race, downtown Indianapolis

Courtesy IWC

45

J. Darrell Bakken

Infiltration gallery, Riverside Station, 1883
Courtesy IWC

46

Riverside Station, c. 1910

Holly-Gaskill pump, Riverside Station

Courtesy IWC

Streetcar to Fairview Park, Courtesy Indianapolis <u>Star</u>

**Canal Boathouse at Fairview park
Courtesy IWC**

Canal bridge at Butler University, 1850s to 1950s

IWC canal patrolman, c. 1910?
Courtesy IWC

IWC canal steamboat at Armstrong Park landing, c. 1890s

Courtesy IWC

HERDRICH AND BOGGS
Certified Public Accountants
901-7 Continental Bank Building
INDIANAPOLIS, IND.
Thursday

9:00 A. M.

The Meriden Case,
    W. B. MILNER, Superintendent Water Works, Birmingham.

9:30 A. M.

Carriage drive for Association's members, starting from the Denison Hotel and including the Water Works.

2:00 P. M.

A Talk,   J. T. FANNING, C. E., Minneapolis.

Litigation of Montgomery, Ala.,
    FRED CROSBY, Superintendent Water Works, Montgomery.

Lowering Water Mains Under Pressure,
    D. W. FRENCH, Deputy Superintendent Hackensack Water Co., Hackensack, N. J.

Asphalt Lining for Old and New Reservoirs,
    L. J. LECONTE, C. E., Oakland, Cal.

8:00 P. M.

Reception for Members and Ladies at the Commercial Club.

SIXTEENTH ANNUAL CONVENTION
OF THE
AMERICAN WATER WORKS ASSOCIATION

INDIANAPOLIS, IND., MAY 26, 27, 28, 1896

ASSOCIATION'S OFFICERS

Acting President
F. A. W. DAVIS . . . . Indianapolis

Vice Presidents
J. CAULFIELD . . . . St. Paul, Minn.
J. A. BOND . . . . Wilmington, Del.
F. CROSBY . . . . Montgomery, Ala.
C. P. ALLEN . . . . Denver, Colo.

Secretary and Treasurer
PETER MILNE . . . . New York City

Commercial Club's Local Committee on Arrangements
    JOHN S. LAZARUS, Chairman
    D. P. ERWIN   F. A. W. DAVIS
    W. M. TAYLOR   EVANS WOOLLEN

The privileges of the Columbia Club, Monument Place, and of the Commercial Club, southwest corner Meridian and Pearl streets, are cordially extended to the Association's members. Guest's cards can be had on application to the information clerk in the Denison Hotel room in which the sessions are held.

ALL SESSIONS, EXCEPT WEDNESDAY EVENING'S,
AT THE DENISON HOTEL.

Tuesday

9:00 A. M.

Convention called to order. Addresses of welcome by GOV. CLAUDE MATTHEWS and MAYOR THOMAS TAGGART.

Address of Acting President, F. A. W. DAVIS, Indianapolis

Resolution on the Death of President W. G. Richards, COL. L. H. GARDNER, Superintendent Water Works, New Orleans.

Question Box.

Water Works and Their Management (continued), L. W. CASE, Superintendent and Secretary Water Works, Detroit.

The Seasonable Fluctuations of Running Streams, ERASTUS G. SMITH, Professor of Chemistry Beloit College, Beloit.

Volunteer Papers.

2:00 P. M.

Report of Committee on Animal and Vegetable Growths Affecting Water Supplies,
    ALBERT R. LEEDS, Professor of Chemistry Stevens Institute of Technology, Hoboken.

Water Supply of Indianapolis, DR. J. N. HURTY, Indianapolis.

A Talk Upon Water Tube Boilers, E. H. WELLS, New York.

Pollution of Streams,   ALBERT BAKER, Indianapolis.

8:00 P. M.

Presentation and Discussion of Subjects not on the programme.

Wednesday

9:00 A. M.

Health Improbable, Economy Impossible Without Filtration and the Meter, J. B. RIDER, C. E., So. Norwalk, Conn.

Out of the Ordinary, JACOB P. DUNN, Editor Sentinel, Indianapolis.

Filtration of Public Water Supplies, ALLEN HAZEN, C. E., Boston.

Our Experience with Automatic Flush Tanks, W. H. LAING, Superintendent Water Works, Racine, Wis.

1:30 P. M.

Carriage drive, starting from the Denison Hotel, and steamboat excursion to the Country Club and Fairview Park for the ladies.

2:00 P. M.

Evil Effects of Politics in Water Works Owned by City Government, W. L. CAMERON, Superintendent Water Works, Kansas City.

Legal Decisions and Legislation, DOW R. GWINN, Superintendent Water Works, Quincy, Ill.

The Best Method of Setting Meters, H. M. LOFTON, Superintendent Water Works, Savannah, Ga.

Laying Water Mains, J. H. DECKER, Deputy Purveyor, D. C. Works, Brooklyn.

8:00 P. M.

At Plymouth Church, S. E. Corner Meridian and New York Streets.

Water Supplies in Egypt, JAMES P. DONAHUE, Secretary and Treasurer, Davenport Water Works, Davenport, Ia.

Water Supply and Distribution, City of Brooklyn (Illustrated), PETER MILNE, C. E., Brooklyn.

Vegetable Growth in Water (Illustrated), STANLEY COULTER, Professor Biology, Purdue University, Lafayette, Ind.

1896 American Water Works Association convention in Indianapolis, including a "steamboat excursion" on the canal "for the ladies"
Courtesy IWC

J. Darrell Bakken

Canal maintenance at West Street, 1907,
with Schissel Bathhouse in background left
Courtesy IWC

CHAPTER 5
CONSULTANTS AND COURT CASES CONFIRM THE CANAL'S VALUE

As the population of Indianapolis multiplied after the turn of the century, consumer demand for water service increased accordingly. During the first four decades of the twentieth century, the Indianapolis Water Company consistently met demand, expanding its surface water supplies and wells, upgrading its treatment and distribution facilities, building pump stations, and even installing customer meters.

Progress involves peaks and valleys

For both the canal and IWC, 1904 was a year of highs and lows. The high point occurred when the company's new White River slow-sand filter plant began processing raw canal water. After grappling with nearly continuous supply problems since the early 1870s, the city now had a low-cost, gravity-fed supply that would provide citizens with ample water service for more than three decades. The canal also continued to drive water-powered pumping at Washington Station.

The death of company president Thomas Morris marked a low point. After twenty-three years of distinguished service to IWC, Morris died at the age of 93. He was succeeded by F. A. W. Davis, who had been treasurer and then vice-president of the company. [86] Other important company leaders during the first two decades of the century were Linnaes C. Boyd and Hugh M. K. Landon, both former executives with Manufacturers' Natural Gas of Indianapolis, who served as officers of IWC until 1912.

Boyd and Landon were principals in an important land acquisition involving the canal. In 1907 IWC purchased the 244-acre Cynthia Butch farm, north of the Woodstock Club and west of Michigan Road. Company archives show that in 1902 F. A. W. Davis retained consulting engineer Joseph H. Dennis to study the lower 152 acres of the farm as a site for an off-canal reservoir. The reservoir was intended to serve as an emergency water supply, in the event of a canal failure above Woodstock, to furnish raw water to the White River filtration plant. The farm was purchased in two sections: IWC paid $30,000 for the lower portion, west of the canal, and Boyd and Landon paid $20,000 for the upper 92 acres, east and south of the canal. The two company officers built homes on their land. The Landon home, Oldfields, was sold to Josiah K. Lilly in 1932. It eventually became part of the Lilly estate and was given to the city for use as an art museum. IWC never built the off-canal reservoir, but it controlled its part of the acreage until 1968 when it donated the tract to the museum. [87]

Another low point of 1904 came when a Fall Creek flood washed out the canal aqueduct—a steel structure, similar in construction to a railroad trestle, that had been installed in 1890. [88] The company replaced the steel construction with a reinforced concrete aqueduct.

During 1907 and 1908 IWC drained the canal below the White River treatment plant in order to remove silt from the canal's downtown section and to install a forebay outlet at Market Street, replacing the original two-level flume used to supply water-wheel contracts. The drainage also allowed for replacement of the three centrifugal turbine-powered pumps at Washington Station. Over the same two-year period, water treatment at the White River plant improved as a result of the addition of a large pre-sedimentation basin.

Consultants Alvord and Metcalf determine the canal's value

In 1909 consulting engineers John W. Alvord of Chicago and Leonard Metcalf of Boston conducted an extensive study of IWC, focusing on the canal's overall value to company operations. The consultants calculated both the value of the water-powered turbines that pumped treated canal water at Washington Station (versus the alternative steam-powered pumps) and the value of 100 percent gravity-powered raw water flow from the canal to the White River treatment plant (versus the theoretical alternative of high-lift pumping from Fall Creek to the west). The report documented twenty-one organizations that were paying IWC's canal department for various water uses, including condensing and steam-making, ice-making, and land rental. [89] Overall, the Alvord and Metcalf report determined that the canal's annual operating income from these uses was $77,000, and its annual operating expenses were $94,332.

The engineers' report also derived the March 31, 1909, IWC and canal reproduction costs for utility valuation and rate-setting purposes. Subtracting accrued depreciation, the engineers concluded that the overall reproduction cost of the canal (including nondepreciated real estate) was $1,634,821. Given IWC's overall 1909 reproduction cost of $8,952,409, this valuation meant that the canal provided 18 percent of the total value of the company and that IWC was the first canal owner to recoup its investment in the canal. [90] In subsequent years, however, the company would have to vigorously defend the canal's valuation— twice before the U.S. Supreme Court and several times before Indiana courts and regulators. [91]

The largest of the twenty-one contracts listed in the Alvord and Metcalf report was a $4,500-per-year contract with Indianapolis Light and Heat Company (later Indianapolis Power and Light) for its Mill Street Station, then located at West 20th Street and North Mill Street. A fifty-year contract, signed in June 1910, provided for canal water to be diverted through an intake approximately 1,000 feet north of the canal's Holton Place gates and then to be conveyed by conduit to and from the condensers of two steam turbines back to the canal. Each steam turbine required 25,500 gallons of water per minute from the canal, more than 36 million gallons per day (mgd) for each turbine. This 72-mgd flow constituted about one third of the canal's typical total flow. No wonder, then, that IWC correspondence frequently registered vigorous complaints when the electric utility delivered water into nearby Fall Creek rather than returning it to the canal. [92]

The canal serves as a theatrical stage

Even as the canal became an increasingly important component of IWC and other Indianapolis businesses, it continued to offer recreational opportunities for local citizens. In Fairview Park, in the summers of 1910 through 1912, a group of Native Americans presented a pageant dramatizing Henry Wadsworth Longfellow's poem "The Song of Hiawatha." The performers erected tepees along the north bank of the canal and floated their canoes in the water. Spectators, for an admission fee of fifty cents, watched from a natural amphitheater on the south bank. Walter B. Hendrickson, in his memoir of his Indiana childhood, recalled the spectacle:

The show was presented at dusk, and the scenes of the poem were placed in an opening in the trees... . The poem was read dramatically by a trained actor, and it was very effective given in the stillness and mystery of the night. The canal became magically the "shining Big-Sea-Water" beside which Nokomis was seated before her tepee ... . At the end, Hiawatha sailed away in a canoe, his white suit and feathered headdress spotlighted, until he disappeared into the world of good spirits. It was a very impressive and realistic play, and we children were deeply stirred. [93]

In 1911 and again in 1912 IWC added one large Delaval electric motor—driven pump to Riverside Station. The company also built a booster pumping station at Broad Ripple in 1912 at the canal inlet and White River.

Clarence Geist purchases IWC

In 1912 Clarence H. Geist, a Pennsylvania businessman, bought IWC from Boyd and Landon. He and his estate would own the company for forty years until the end of 1952. For the first four months of his ownership, Geist also served as company president, but because of a state law requiring officers of Indiana public utilities to live in Indiana, Clarence L. Kirk took over the post until 1917. In that year Geist was able to return as company president and remained in that position until his death in 1938. [94]

A major flood temporarily interrupts water service

One of the greatest challenges to the company's use and maintenance of the canal, its water supply, and pumping stations came in March 1913. Early in the morning of Easter Sunday, March 23, a downpour of rain began and continued until Monday morning. By that time both White River and Fall Creek were rising rapidly—the river "two inches an hour all morning." By the time the Indianapolis *News* went to press on Tuesday, March 25, flooding had brought the city to a standstill. Utilities were cut off, and the streetcars and trains had stopped running. Water had risen twelve feet above the Broad Ripple Dam, and the northern half of that town was flooded; only the canal bridge was preventing water from flooding the southern half as well. The canal's banks had broken at Riverside Amusement Park, inundating the land and the park's facilities. Washington Street Station was already under water and had been out of commission since the previous night. By noon two feet of water surrounded the buildings at Riverside Station, the result of a break in the Fall Creek levee at Indiana Avenue. Workers were forced to abandon the pumps at 12:30 p.m., and all water service to the city was cut off. On Wednesday one of the main bridges over White River, at West Washington Street, collapsed at both ends because of pressure from the debris-filled water rushing against it.

Although IWC told the public it hoped to restore some water service within the next day or two, on Thursday a local newspaper published a list of wells where residents could obtain safe drinking water. Finally, on Friday, Riverside Station resumed pumping water through company mains. Even then, startup was problematic because the main flywheel of one pump was still in six feet of water. When the wheel started to turn, it threw up so much water that workers had to turn off the pump engine until they could remove more water from the floor of the station. By afternoon two of the large pumps were operating, but the third pump in the Davis building was still flooded.

On Saturday a *News* headline read "Water Pressure is Coming to Normal—Fire Protection Assured Most of City by Big Pumps at Riverside Station." IWC had managed to restore distribution system water pressure to 22 pounds (40 to 45 was normal) with its two main Riverside pumps, but the West Washington Station would be unusable for many days. By Monday, a week after the flood began, the company had its filter beds at White River working and was pumping clean water through the mains, although it still warned customers of the need to boil water. A front-page editorial cartoon in the *News* reinforced the message with a sketch of a huge black cauldron full of boiling liquid and the caption "Keep the Pot Boiling." According to the newspaper, IWC was "employing all the laborers it [could] find" to repair breeches in and damage to the canal from Broad Ripple all the way south to downtown Indianapolis. [95]

IWC's customer base tops 300,000

In 1914, to meet growing demand in northeast Indianapolis, IWC constructed new wells, the water system's first underground storage reservoir, and the first high-lift pump station at what is now Fall Creek Station. At the end of that year, annual average water consumption was 23.3 mgd. By 1920 IWC served almost 320,000 city residents, and consumption reached 30.2 mgd. To meet demand, the company installed a DeLaval 30-mgd high-lift pump to replace Riverside Station's old Holly-Gaskill pump of 1889.

Metcalf recommends customer metering and more pumping capacity

In 1921 Geist and Kirk re-engaged consulting engineer Metcalf, coauthor of the 1909 valuation report, for a comprehensive engineering study of the entire IWC drinking water system. The study also reviewed regulation, rate of return, and company finances. An eleven-page report, "The Future Water Service of the City of Indianapolis," appeared in June 1923. The study's analysis and recommendations looked forward fifteen years to 1937. Among Metcalf's recommendations were: metering of all service connections, a new 12-mgd rapid-sand filter plant at White River, an impounding reservoir for a new surface water supply on either White River or Fall Creek, increasing high-lift pumping capacity, and a major distribution system upgrade. The total cost of these improvements amounted to almost $8 million.

IWC confronts court battles over rates

Through much of 1923 IWC was involved in local, state, and federal legal proceedings. On March 23 the Public Service Commission of Indiana (PSCI) ruled that IWC, by resolution of its board of directors, must surrender its water utility franchise, granted by the city council in 1870, and accept an indeterminate PSCI permit. This permit gave the state, rather than the city, the authority to approve water rates and to regulate the utility.

In June company president Geist hosted a dinner party at the Claypool Hotel for "over 400 state and local office holders, bankers, businessmen, and labor representatives." The purpose of the party was to introduce a new general manager to those assembled. Geist also used the occasion to inform his guests that IWC was about to request a 20 percent rate increase from the PSCI because the cost of the improvements outlined in Metcalf's report appeared to necessitate higher customer water rates. [96]

For the company's summer 1923 rate case, counsel Albert Baker of Baker and Daniels filed with PSCI a twenty-six—page memorandum entitled "Judicial and Legislative History of the Central Canal." The document summarized state canal laws from 1835 to 1923, confirming that the company continued to hold fee-simple title to all of its canal land and that the company had the right to use the canal for city water supply and not just the original uses of transportation and mill power. [97]

Later this same year the U.S. Supreme Court, citing the PSCI decision, ruled that "the entire canal property is used and useful in the performance of service this utility was created to perform." After the court's verdict, the PSCI approved a 12 percent rate increase in late 1923, but the city took this decision to court. Three years later, in November 1926, the U.S. Supreme Court finally ruled in the case of *McCardle* v. *Indianapolis Water Company*, finding in the company's favor. [98]

During and after the court cases, IWC began to invest in the improvements Metcalf had recommended: a rapid sand filter plant at White River Station in 1926, a high-service electric pump at Washington Station in 1927, major distribution main additions (especially for fire protection), and universal metering. In 1927 the company had to restore Washington Station after a tornado destroyed the pump station's front section. In the late 1920s the company was also forced to begin dealing with slippage along parts of the canal bank, first in the spring of 1926 at the high bluff area just upstream from Michigan Road. Similar repairs also took place in 1928 and again in 1935. [99]

Company fortunes were affected by the economic downturn that began in 1929. In 1930 total water consumption had reached 34.54 mgd (an increase from 30.2 mgd in 1920), and the population IWC served had increased from 319,800 to 371,500. Despite continued population increases during the 1930s, however, consumption would not exceed this amount until 1941. IWC did continue to improve and expand its citywide system. In the late 1920s and the 1930s the company acquired land for and designed

Geist Reservoir, its first impounding reservoir, and Fall Creek Station, a pumping station as well as IWC's second major rapid-sand filter plant. The company also kept up its commitment to universal metering. In 1932 two of old water-powered mills in front of Washington Station were razed, leaving Beveridge Paper, located next to the station, as one of the few remaining canal water customers from the nineteenth century. [100]

In addition to the economy, another deterrent to IWC planning and expansion in the 1930s was a serious, long-running dispute over water rates that again involved the company, PSCI, and the city. The commission allowed a rate increase in 1932, but the city appealed. After negotiations, IWC and the city agreed on rate increases for large customers, such as real estate developers, and a reduction of minimum monthly charges for residential customers. A group of developers sued and won their own rate reduction, provoking a company appeal to federal court. Appeals dragged on until May 1938, when the U.S. Supreme Court approved a large two-year improvement program for the company. An essential part of the decision was affirmation of the canal's valuation as "used and useful." [101]

With the increased revenue accrued as a result of the Supreme Court decision, IWC completed its 16-mgd Fall Creek rapid sand filter plant, a second elevated water storage tank, and improvements to its pumping and distribution systems. In 1941, at the outset of World War II, IWC was well positioned to meet the future water demands of a rapidly growing city, thanks in large part to the financial advantages afforded by the canal.

CHAPTER 6
THE CITY RECEIVES THE LOWER CANAL AS A GIFT

In December 1941 the United States entered World War II, declaring war on Japan December 10 and on Germany and Italy December 11. As the decade began, the city of Indianapolis and IWC were putting the depression years behind them and preparing to meet the needs of population growth and wartime industrial expansion. [102] Fortunately, IWC's rate base and its water rates from the PSCI (based on the court battles of the 1920s and 1930s) allowed the company to finance its second major surface water supply source, Geist Reservoir, and its second major water treatment plant and pumping station at Fall Creek Station. The three facilities were completed in 1942 and 1943, allowing water service to keep pace with the city's growth. IWC's service population increased from 401,000 customers in 1940 to 445,000 in 1945. During those same years, water consumption rose from 32.75 million gallons per day (mgd) to 48.5 mgd.

Other company facilities experienced more modest improvements during the 1940s. The only major work at White River Station was completion of several shallow wells in a sand and gravel formation around the station grounds. These wells provided standby and emergency water supplies.

Industrial use and neighborhoods along the canal decline

The amount of canal water used for industrial purposes continued to decrease. In 1936 IWC had only eight industrial customers; by 1944 the number had dwindled to five. The primary remaining industrial uses for canal water were cooling and ice-making. [103] Indianapolis Power and Light's Mill Street Station, according to a 1946 contract, required 25,500 gallons per minute of cooling water for each of its two turbines. For these 72 mgd of canal water, the power company paid about $250 each month. [104]

Neighborhoods along the canal were also changing. Housing conditions were deteriorating along the section of the canal that began at about Michigan Street at the northwest edge of the downtown business district and continued north of 16th Street. When photographer and poet James Fox recorded life in Indianapolis during the 1930s, he produced what might have been idyllic pictures of children fishing along the canal had it not been for "stark images of ... dilapidated structures, outdoor pumps, and trash" in the background. One of Fox's poems, "View From a Bicycle," reflected the contrasts:

> I saw the Canal running placidly through the city.
> Leaves floated gracefully, slowly turning.
> People threw garbage into it.
> Flotsam drifted like little boats set afloat.

This residential decline would continue unabated for years. Much of the downtown business district along the canal also became "unkempt" and "blighted." [105]

IWC expands its service area past the city limits

In 1947 IWC began to expand its services outside the city limits of Indianapolis, building the Rockville Booster Station to serve new areas in western Marion County and the South Booster Station to serve new customers in Southport and Homecroft. Simultaneously, the company was expanding its network of water mains toward the county line in the same directions. In 1948 the second half of the Fall Creek treatment plant went into service. By 1950 total water consumption by all of IWC's customers reached 53.35 mgd. [106]

New IWC owner builds second impounding reservoir

In 1951 the company added another 36-mgd rapid sand filter plant at White River. Rumors in the city indicated that IWC was planning a second impounding reservoir for an additional surface water supply, this one northwest of Noblesville in Hamilton County. But in 1952 other news temporarily delayed debate over a second reservoir—the Murchison brothers, Clint Jr. and John, of Dallas, Texas, bought IWC. [107] The following year the new owners filed for a 33 percent rate increase, primarily to cover the $6.5 million cost of a new reservoir. One of the primary reasons for building the reservoir was to augment the guaranteed water supply from the canal and the White River, a step the company deemed necessary because of ever-increasing customer demand (consumption had reached 63.07 mgd by the end of 1955). The rate case spent months in the courts, and finally in January 1956 the state supreme court ruled for the company. When Morse Reservoir was placed into service, it tripled the yield of the White River system from 25 mgd to 75 mgd. This higher yield also increased the value of the canal and its raw water conveyance to the White River filter plant. [108]

As IWC was expanding its supply sources in the 1950s and looking to the future, part of the canal's past was coming to an end. In 1955 the company removed from service the last high bridge over the canal, adjacent to Butler University (previously the location of Fairview Park until 1922). The bridge, with five feet of clearance between the water surface and the bottom of the bridge planks, was the last bridge of the original design that allowed canal flatboats and barges pulled by teams of horses to move freely beneath it. [109]

The canal continues to be valuable despite necessary repairs

Even with two reservoirs now serving the company, the canal continued to be an essential asset to IWC. According to a May 1958 newspaper article, A. M. Rife, a Philadelphia engineer who was a witness during an IWC rate case, testified that the entire canal was both used and useful for rate-making purposes. Rife calculated that by water utility valuation standards of the day, the cost of the original canal would be nearly three quarters of a million dollars, with a reproduction cost of more than $2.5 million and a total valuation of $3,842,539. [110]

In April 1963 a major slippage occurred in a half-mile portion of the canal embankment along the High Banks section of the old towpath just upstream from Michigan Road. Lesser slippages had already occurred in this section six times between 1926 and 1961. Even the original surveyors in 1835 had predicted problems with this portion of the canal, noting in their report to the state legislature that the "chief obstacles to the construction of a canal" were "the bluffs or washed banks ... mostly of clay ... [that] vary in height from 30 to 60 feet." [111]

IWC commissioned two civil engineering professors from Purdue University to study the problem at the High Banks. They reported that the slippage had occurred in two sections of the embankment, each about 250 to 300 feet long. Along each section "the towpath had slumped down about 2 feet ... and had moved several inches towards the river." After four years of study, the professors produced a written report recommending a network of surveying stations, a system of borings for piezometers that would measure water levels in the embankments, and the placement of additional riprap in selected locations. By adopting the report's recommendations and assigning company personnel to routinely monitor and patrol the canal banks, IWC was able to prevent another major problem in the area until 1992. [112]

New pump station raises distribution system pressure

A major new pumping station went into service in 1961, adjacent to the White River filter plant. In 1963 the company replaced the last steam-driven pumps at Riverside Station with new electric motor-driven pumps. Together, these two stations raised distribution system water pressure downtown so significantly that in 1964 IWC began to study the possibility of abandoning and selling the entire downtown portion of the canal below the intake

65

of the White River filter plant, as well as Washington Station.

IWC negotiates with the city regarding a downtown inner-loop highway

While the company was conducting its study, the state and city were considering a proposal for an inner-loop interstate highway system around the downtown area. The model specified three expensive bridges across the canal just north of West 11th Street. If the canal and Washington Station were to be abandoned, however, those bridges could be replaced by more economical highway structures. IWC stepped up the pace of its study and in September 1965 sent a letter to the state highway commission, informing it of the company's intent to abandon the lower canal by early 1969.

Negotiations between the company and the city were lengthy and complex. Because the canal intersected the northwest corner of the proposed interstate loop and the model specified no western leg of the highway, IWC first offered the lower canal land to the city for a west leg thoroughfare, a proposal that would have allowed a complete, four-sided interstate-quality inner loop. The canal land was appraised, and IWC offered to sell its portion from about 11th Street to Ohio Street for $350,000. Despite city council promises to give the matter serious consideration, the first governmental response came almost two years later through a July 1967 report from the city—county planning commission. The report cited several possible uses for the downtown portion of the canal, stressing its potential for urban beautification, but did not in any way deal with its relationship to transportation planning. Newspaper editorials from 1967 and 1968 echoed the theme of aesthetics, suggesting the canal's usefulness for public recreation and city beautification. [113]

In October 1968 an Indianapolis Regional Transportation and Development Study (IRTADS) proposed to use the canal right-of-way from the inner loop's northwest leg south to Washington Street for a below-ground-level busway or transitway. At the same time as this study, a mayoral task force considered incorporating the canal into a master plan for its urban university, Indiana University Purdue University of Indianapolis (IUPUI). The task force proposed a canal park and adjacent property developments as well as a new southern end point for the canal, south of the existing terminus at Washington Station. In March 1969 IWC gave the task force its official reply, citing terms and conditions for sale of the canal land. [114]

While negotiations dragged on, the company retired Washington Station from service on April 1, 1969—almost 98 years after its pumps were first activated. And through another landmark event, IWC's exclusive ownership of the canal lands from Broad Ripple all the way south to Washington Station ceased when the state of Indiana purchased two sections of land (one south of West 38th Street for a White River crossing and the other at the northwest corner of the inner loop) for the construction of Interstate 65.

By early 1970 IWC and the city still had not resolved the planning issues related to the lower canal. Company president Thomas W. Moses, with characteristic understatement, wrote to deputy mayor John Walls, expressing frustration with more than six years of fruitless discussion:

I am enclosing a story of our dealings with various public authorities on the lower canal. I think it is rather interesting and not a little amusing.

There is really no rush about this, but I would appreciate having the current thinking on possible use of this land. [115]

In January 1971, almost a year later, Mayor Richard G. Lugar replied to the company's inquiries, suggesting that IWC consider making a gift of the lower canal and related properties to the city. Moses answered favorably, and through deeds signed in 1972 and 1973 the company placed most of the lower canal, divided into three parcels of land, into a trust, until the city could take title.

The donation was appraised at a value of $401,849. Eventually, in 1976, Mayor William H. Hudnut III notified the company that the city was taking over title of the canal land and properties. This left IWC holding 6.55 miles of the original Central Canal. [116]

White River Station and the canal, c. 1920s

Slow sand filter plant, White River Station

Canal aqueduct, 1890

Canal aqueduct, 1890

Failure of 1890 aqueduct in 1904

Courtesy IWC

View of failure of aqueduct masonry, 1904

New Fall Creek canal aqueduct, 1905

Courtesy IWC

Water-powered mill at Washington Street

THE WATER LANDMARK AWARD

After a *Century of Water Supply Service*, on August 11, 1971, the Indianapolis Water Company Canal (18th Street to White River at Broad Ripple) is being officially designated as an Historic Water Landmark by the American Water Works Association.

This award, established in 1967, honors such "tangible, physical property that has, or had, a direct relationship with water supply, treatment, distribution or technological development. . . .and sufficient age to have established significance as a Landmark and must be so recognized within the community in which it is located".

An American Water Landmark must be approved and accepted by an appropriate government body or a water utility and be maintained in a manner consistent with its significance.

The Central Canal -- the Indianapolis Water Company Canal -- assuredly meets all prerequisites and joins these other Water Landmarks previously dedicated by the American Water Works Association:

Chicago Water Tower, Chicago, Illinois
Theodore Roosevelt Dam, Salt River Project,
          Phoenix, Arizona
High Bridge Water Tower, New York City
Old Mission Dam and Flume, San Diego, Calif.
North Point Water Tower, Milwaukee, Wisconsin
Water Tower at Borman Park, Gary, Indiana
Riverside Water Tower, Riverside, Illinois
Los Angeles Aqueduct Cascades
          Los Angeles, California

DEDICATION PROGRAM

10:50 A.M.   Convene
(EST)   Krannert Pavilion, West Plaza
              Indianapolis Museum of Art
              1200 West 38th Street

11:00 A.M.   Presiding . . . Leo Louis, *Chairman*
              Water Landmarks Committee,
              Indiana Section, American Water
              Works Association; Past President,
              AWWA; President, Gary-Hobart Water
              Corporation, Gary, Indiana

              Opening Remarks and Introductions

              Welcome to
              Indianapolis Museum of Art
              Carl J. Weinhardt, Jr., *Director*

              Significance of the Central Canal
              in the History of Indianapolis
              George S. Diener, *Chairman*
              Indianapolis Sesquicentennial Commission

              Recognition of the Central Canal for its
              Century of Service as a Vital Part of
              the Indianapolis Water System
              Richard G. Lugar
              Mayor of Indianapolis

              Designation of the Central Canal as an
              American Water Landmark
              Thurston E. Larson, *Immediate Past President,*
              American Water Works Association; Head,
              Chemistry Section, State Water Survey,
              Urbana, Illinois

              Acceptance of
              American Water Landmark Designation
              Thomas W. Moses
              Chairman of the Board and President
              Indianapolis Water Company

11:40 A.M.   Reception
              Alliance Garden Pavilion, West Terrace
              Indianapolis Museum of Art

12:15 P.M.   Luncheon
              Alliance Garden Pavilion

1:15 P.M.   Tour of the Indianapolis Museum of Art

AWWA Historical Water Landmark
Courtesy IWC

Courtesy Butler University

Hiawatha pageant along the canal at Fairview Park

1913 flood damage to canal at Monon bridge, Broad Ripple

1913 flood damage adjacent to canal, Broad Ripple

Courtesy IWC

"Break in bank of canal, 1913"

Canal bank breach north of 30th Street, 1913

Speedway Avenue and Riverside Station after 1913 flood

Courtesy IWC

White River bridge, Washington Street, after 1913 flood

Washington Station Reconstruction, Rear View, 1917, East, Courtesy IWC

Washington Station Reconstruction, Rear View, 1917, West, Courtesy IWC

1865 Water-Powered Mill Demolished

Courtesy Indianapolis <u>Star</u>

Near-Downtown Canal (1930), Courtesy HLFI

J. Darrell Bakken

Downtown Canal at night

Courtesy O. James Fox and Indiana Historical Society

REFLECTIONS IN THE CANAL.
Text and Drawing by Frederick Polley.

This sketch was made on one of the hottest days in August, but I've tried to express in it a feeling of a quiet day, placidly smooth-flowing water, traffic nil, and gossip at a standstill instead of heat and humidity. In my walk from the canal gates, where the waters disappear into an underground channel, to the West street concrete bridge I noticed only three persons actually working and I have my doubts about two of them. One of these, a man, was cleaning rubbish and driftwood from the canal. He labored slowly and methodically. The beating rays of an August sun constrained him to an easy, slothful pottering. A certain sleepy perseverance shadowed the activities of the two women who sat on the footboards and fished silently.

Over in the park, Military park, all was quiet. The shrill whistle of the ice cream vendor died on the heat waves for want of active response. The benches were well filled, but most of the occupants were asleep. One fellow who had removed his shoes to air-condition his feet kept eyeing me with my pencil and pad, but I gave him a reassuring nod.

Reflections in water are most interesting. Usually the reflected image is darker than the object that casts the reflection. This is true when the water is smooth and glasslike. Flowing water, or wind-rippled water, breaks up the reflected image and it becomes tremorous and wriggly, taking on fascinating forms and mysterious shapes. It's great fun watching, if you're not in a hurry.

Play is often the prelude to work and well you should heed it. Work is play, too, if you know how to turn the trick. The transition should be unconscious, harmonious. Work of the highest quality should evoke interest, freshness, vitality and mental spontaneity. These are characteristics that are present in play and in games.

1937 Canal Sketch in Indianapolis Star, Courtesy Indianapolis Star

J. Darrell Bakken

West 16th Street Aerial Looking Southeast Down Indiana Av., 1955
Courtesy Indianapolis <u>News</u>

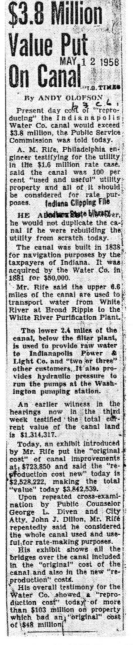

$3.8 Million Value Put On Canal

MAY 1 2 1958

'T.S. TIMES

By ANDY OLOFSON

Present day cost of "reproducing" the Indianapolis Water Co. canal would exceed $3.8 million, the Public Service Commission was told today.

A. M. Rife, Philadelphia engineer testifying for the utility in the $1.6 million rate case, said the canal was 100 per cent "used and useful" utility property and all of it should be considered for rate purposes.

HE Added, however, he would not duplicate the canal if he were rebuilding the utility from scratch today.

The canal was built in 1838 for navigation purposes by the taxpayers of Indiana. It was acquired by the Water Co. in 1881 for $50,000.

Mr. Rife said the upper 6.6 miles of the canal are used to transport water from White River at Broad Ripple to the White River Purification Plant.

The lower 2.4 miles of the canal, below the filter plant, is used to provide raw water to Indianapolis Power & Light Co. and "two or three" other customers. It also provides hydraulic pressure to run the pumps at the Washington pumping station.

An earlier witness in the hearings now in the third week testified the total current value of the canal land is $1,314,317.

Today, an exhibit introduced by Mr. Rife put the "original cost" of canal improvements at $723,850 and said the "reproduction cost new" today is $2,528,222, making the total "value" today $3,842,539.

Upon repeated cross-examination by Public Counselor George L. Diven and City Atty. John J. Dillon, Mr. Rife repeatedly said he considered the whole canal used and useful for rate-making purposes.

His exhibit shows all the bridges over the canal included in the "original" cost of the canal and also in the new "reproduction" costs.

His overall testimony for the Water Co. showed a "reproduction cost" today of more than $103 million on property which had an "original" cost of $48 million.

Canal Value in 1958 Rate Case

Canal Historic Marker, Meridian Street
Courtesy IWC

Washington Station (circa 1950's)
Courtesy IWC

View of the pond behind the Indianapolis Museum of Art.
from Indianapolis: A Pictorial History, Edward A. Leary, p. 180

Courtesy IMA

J. Darrell Bakken

Dedication of Canal as Historic Water Landmark
Left to right: Mayor Richard Lugar; Roll Mc Laughlin, historian; Thomas
Moses, IWC; Leo Louis, AWWA

Courtesy IWC

CENTRAL CANAL CHRONOLOGY

1836: The Indiana Internal Improvement Program bill, passed by the General Assembly and signed by Governor Noah Noble on January 27, included construction of the Indiana Central Canal to connect the Wabash and Erie Canal between Peru and Worthington.

1839: The Indianapolis Division of the Central Canal was formally opened on June 27 for transportation from Broad Ripple to Indianapolis as well as supplying water power to various mills.

1851: The State of Indiana sold the Canal to private persons, and it passed successively through many ownerships, both individual and corporate.

' *1871:* The Canal, purchased by the Water Works Company of Indianapolis, was first used on June 1 to power hydraulic pumps at Washington Station to distribute water from wells to customers.

1881: The Indianapolis Water Company, incorporated April 23, purchased its predecessor company at sheriff's sale and became the owner of the Central Canal.

1904: Water from the Canal, taken from White River at Broad Ripple, was first used to supply water for treatment at the White River Purification Plant north of 18th Street. The water then went by conduit to Riverside Pumping Station and the original Washington Station (inactive since 1969). The Canal north of 18th Street continues to provide the major portion of water supply for distribution to Indianapolis and the company's growing service area.

' *1971: Start of a Second Century*
of Water Supply Service

DEDICATION
of the
Indiana
CENTRAL CANAL
as an
American Water Landmark
by the
American Water Works
Association

August 11, 1971

Placement of plaque
Indianapolis Museum of Art

Canal Named AWWA Historic Water Landmark
Courtesy IWC

CHAPTER 7
IWC CELEBRATES A CENTURY AND MORE OF CANAL OWNERSHIP

In 1976 the Indianapolis Water Company contributed the lower 2.25 miles of the canal and Washington Station to the city, eliminating a significant public relations problem—an open, unused, and unsightly canal. IWC also benefitted from making the bequest, taking a corporate tax deduction for the modest salvage value of slightly more than $400,000 and freeing more of its resources to develop new water supplies and other facilities for its ever-increasing customer base. [117]

Canal operation and maintenance concerns were now mostly a matter of routine: monitoring the High Banks slide area; patrolling the length of the towpath; repairing damage to the canal banks in and near Broad Ripple (caused by the large number of wild and domestic water fowl living along this section of the canal); and, occasionally, performing minor maintenance on old canal structures and embankments.

IWC continued to own legal right-of-way for the entire operating length of the canal. Any new canal crossing agreements—with the state, the city, private contractors, or other utilities—still required a permit from the company. Of particular concern to IWC were permits for construction of sanitary and storm sewers that involved cutting through the clay seal along the bottom of the canal. When such permits were issued, they required special resealing of the canal's bottom surface with bentonite in order to prevent water leakage into the underlying sand and gravel.

In April 1981 the company celebrated its one hundredth anniversary, as well as one century of canal ownership. The next year Carmel, Indiana, businessman Robert Hoffman proposed reviving a long-absent use for canal water—excursion boating. Basing his proposal on tour boats in use along a downtown stretch of canal in San Antonio, Texas, Hoffman requested IWC's permission to operate four 24-passenger shallow boats that would take 90-minute sightseeing trips along the canal in the Broad Ripple area. The plans, however, soon ran into difficulties. IWC was worried that the boats would not be able to operate safely, given the low bridge clearances on that section of the canal. Possible pollution of the company's primary drinking water supply was another factor, as was IWC's potential legal liability if any passengers were injured. Hoffman's plans were never realized. [118]

IWC increases its surface supplies' dependable yield

Beginning in July 1979 the company conducted several engineering studies to confirm the dependable yield of its primary surface water supply, which included Morse Reservoir, White River, and the canal. In cooperation with the U.S. Geological Survey and the Indiana Department of Natural Resources, IWC measured seepage through the clay bottom of the canal into the underlying sand-and-gravel outwash. After 140 years of canal use, the amount of seepage was negligible. Based on this study, as well as a study of the volume and dependable yield of Morse Reservoir and a 1985 summary report, IWC was able to increase its surface water dependable yield from 75 to 87 million gallons per day (mgd) and create an important source of supply for its planned fourth water treatment plant, White River North (completed in 1991). [119]

Another breach occurs along the canal's High Banks

In 1992 history repeated itself along the High Banks portion of the canal. A breach of the riverside canal bank—the first since the 1913 flood—occurred early Friday morning, June 19. On Wednesday a violent thunderstorm had brought several inches of rain and extremely high winds, and the storm had continued until Thursday morning. Thirty hours later an IWC employee discovered a canal breach almost 100 feet long in the High Banks area near Butler University. Virtually all of the canal's water flow from Broad Ripple upstream from the break, as well as water from the canal's south end at White River Station, was rushing through the break. Ultimately, the bottom of the canal was eroded along a length of 150 feet from depths of 4 to 6 feet. The breach had occurred when storm winds blew down trees vertically toward the river. The trees' roots were embedded in banks already softened by heavy rain; when the roots were upended, they removed enough of the bank to allow canal water to escape into the river.

By 8 o'clock Friday morning, IWC personnel were already on site. After conferring with state, city, and university representatives, as well as two private contractors, the company took action. White River treatment plant had lost all of its supply, and every high-lift pump station in the system had been affected. The company maximized the output of all its other sources and asked customers to conserve water until the canal could be repaired. The breach was filled with vertical steel piling, compacted clay was installed on both sides of the piling, and the eroded canal bottom was also filled with compacted clay. By Sunday afternoon three hundred loads of soil and clay had been trucked down a temporary access road. Very early Monday morning the canal was filled with water, and all IWC treatment plants and pumping stations resumed normal operations before sunrise. [120]

IWC becomes a subsidiary of an electric and gas utility

Another chapter in the history of the canal began in March 1997, when IWC became a wholly owned subsidiary of Northern Indiana Public Service Company (NIPSCO) of Merrillville, an electric and gas utility. Under this owner, IWC continued to expand its groundwater supply and added two more high-lift pumping stations to the system.

New bridges and trails give the canal a face-lift

During the 1990s the appearance of several portions of the canal was improved, along with a number of its structures. Butler University built a wooden footbridge over the canal in Holcomb

Gardens. In Broad Ripple the city removed a 1950s parking structure that had straddled the canal along Westfield Boulevard. Local groups joined together to construct a footbridge over the canal at College Avenue and to reconstruct an 1873 bridge (originally from Montgomery County) as another footbridge at Illinois Street. Another salvaged footbridge from Montgomery County went up on the terraces of the Indianapolis Museum of Art, connecting the museum with the lake and garden to the west. A Greenways Monon Trail used by bicyclists and walkers began at the Monon bridge over the canal on Westfield Boulevard.

A new century brings more growth

According to the 2000 U.S. Census, the population of Indianapolis and Marion County was 860,454. IWC was serving well over 800,000 of these people. The company's water customers consumed 134.74 mgd in 2000, up 15 percent from 1990 consumption levels. IWC's service area now included towns in Marion, Morgan, Hendricks, Hancock and Montgomery counties. [121]

As the new century began, the canal continued to be an asset both to the city (as described in Chapter 8) and to IWC. In 2000, the company saved an estimated $400,000 in raw water pumping costs, thanks to gravity flow through the canal to the White River treatment plant. [122] If total pumping costs saved over the ninety-five years that the canal was used to convey public water supply could be calculated, the savings would amount to millions of dollars.

The new century also brought changes to IWC, whose parent company, NiSource (formerly NIPSCO) offered IWC for sale by order of the U.S. Securities and Exchange Commission. On April 30, 2002, the city of Indianapolis officially purchased the company, ending a long history of private ownership, but also returning the Water Company portion of the old Central Canal to local ownership.

CHAPTER 8
RESTORING THE LOWER CANAL
REVITALIZES DOWNTOWN INDIANAPOLIS

From 1964 to 1976 Indianapolis Water Company worked with the city and state to create a positive future for the lower central canal (the portion below West 20th Street that the company no longer used or found useful). [123] The subsequent twenty-five-year rehabilitation of the lower canal was the most economically and culturally significant project ever undertaken along the length of the Central Canal.

First, IWC contacted the state highway department, offering to sell the portion of the canal that began at the northwest corner of Interstate Highway 65 as it entered the downtown area. The company then offered to sell the lower canal to the city to be used as the fourth leg of the inner loop formed by Interstates 65 and 70 on the north, east, and south edges of downtown. When neither of these options were accepted, the company again offered to sell the lower canal to the city but this time as the east anchor of what was to become a redeveloped urban area for IUPUI. In January 1971, the young city—county government of Mayor Lugar asked IWC to donate the lower canal to the city, and during 1972 and 1973 the company placed the land below West 20th Street in trust for "park and recreational" uses. On November 24, 1976, the city took formal title to Washington Station; title to the lower canal was accepted on December 27. [124]

Planning for restoration of the lower canal land begins

City planning for the best use of the newly acquired land began in 1972, when a twenty-two—person Waterways Task Force was created by the Greater Indianapolis Progress Committee, a group that had been a major force in downtown revitalization during the 1960s and 1970s. [125] The task force's study of the lower canal was one of the first major downtown planning efforts of Uni-Gov under Mayor Lugar. Unfortunately, the 1974 report, prepared by a

Texas consulting group, was not accepted locally because it proposed high excavation, reconstruction, and redevelopment costs and because it threatened to damage historic Military Park. [126]

The Historic Landmarks Foundation of Indiana (HLFI), which had a representative on the Waterways Task Force, proposed that the lower central canal be studied as a potential historic district. Foundation staff, aided by state, city, university, and private consultants, issued their own report in September 1975. [127] This report examined the lower central canal from the perspective of historic preservation and noted that comparable canal projects in other cities not only constituted important preservation accomplishments but also had achieved positive economic effects. [128]

The HLFI report identified a canal corridor (soon to be named the Canal Walk) between West Street and Senate Avenue as the central feature between two principal development areas, IUPUI northwest of West Street and the State Office Building to the east and south. The canal and Military Park were also considered key to redevelopment west of the bridge at West and Market streets. In contrast to the massive reconstruction proposed by the 1974 report, the foundation report recommended "development of the Lower Central Canal as an urban linear park." HLFI recommended conserving the traditional canal configuration and rehabilitating and reusing as many existing features as possible. The obvious benefit was a reduction in estimated cost, from more than $20 million for the 1974 proposal to less than $10 million for the new plan. It would the city take several years, however, to obtain even this level of funding.

Redevelopment projects get under way

The city's Department of Metropolitan Development (DMD) and the Indianapolis Historic Preservation Commission were designated coordinators for all canal corridor planning. The first major project was the Northwest Redevelopment Project Urban Renewal Plan of 1982. Its purposes were to eliminate blight, provide area improvements, stimulate economic development, encourage historic preservation, prevent further decline of the city center, and create downtown jobs. The plan created three redevelopment subdistricts—Midtown/MEDIC (the Midtown Economic Development & Industrial Corporation), Canal Walk, and Lockefield Gardens. It also identified potential land uses and accelerated land acquisition (the last acquisitions of land adjacent to the canal). [129]

By early 1985 DMD had received both design guidelines for the Canal Walk corridor (from West Street to Ohio Street to St. Clair Street) and $7.9 million from the Urban Mass Transit Administration to fund initial construction. The federal mass-transit funds, designated for renovation and improvement of historic transportation facilities, needed to be matched by both public agency expenditures (by the Indianapolis Department of Transportation and the State Office Building Commission) and private funds (from the Lilly Endowment and the Indianapolis Foundation). In 1983 the city's transportation department had already constructed a new West Street Bridge, allowing this section of the canal to be lowered and the adjacent land to be redeveloped. The State Office Building Commission worked to ensure that the canal pool and fountain at West and Ohio Streets (adjacent to the state office building) would become the first project and the centerpiece of Canal Walk redevelopment.

The section of the canal just west of the West Street Bridge was temporarily diverted underground through a 54-inch conduit to provide an overflow for excess Canal Walk water until work on a new lower conduit could be completed all the way to White River. The project's second phase, begun in the summer of 1986, included lowering the original canal from the West Street Bridge to New York Street, excavating the Ohio Street basin adjacent to the north State Office Building, building a new water pump and piping system, and constructing the concrete Ohio Street basin and appurtenances. The canal project added sidewalks and lighting as far north as Michigan Street and the city built a new fire station, number 13, at the corner of Ohio and West streets.

Subsequent phases of the project brought the addition of a Vermont Street pedestrian bridge and a west-side turnaround adjacent to the bridge, as well as concrete lining of additional sections of the canal and an extensive landscaping effort. [130] In August 1999 a survivors' memorial to the crew of the U.S.S. *Indianapolis* was dedicated on the Walnut Street commons along the Canal Walk. Reconstruction north of St. Clair Street to Interstate 65 at 11th Street was completed in May 2001. [131]

In the area bounded by Ohio Street, Senate Avenue, West 11th Street, and West Street, construction projects along the Canal Walk now include a motel, five apartment and condominium complexes, three office buildings, two churches, a state parking garage, a Science and Technology Center, and the headquarters for several organizations, including the Historic Landmarks Foundation, Girls Inc., the American College of Sports Medicine, and the Indiana Historical Society. The MEDIC area, which has been developed all the way to West 11th Street and Fall Creek, includes a new IUPUI law school at the corner of New York and West streets. [132]

The state helps to restore its former property

The story of the restoration of the lower central canal is also a story of planning and development by the canal's original owner— the state of Indiana. The city deeded a half-mile-plus portion of the canal (the section west of the West Street Bridge to White River) to the White River State Park Commission in October 1980. [133] Planning for renovation of Washington Pumping Station at the White River end of the canal had already begun the previous year. The state proposed that the pumphouse, as it was renamed, become the White River State Park Commission's headquarters and the park information/visitors center. In July 1980 the building was added to the National Register of Historic Places. Private donations made the restoration possible, and state park staff moved in to their pumphouse offices August 31, 1981. In November 1982 the American Water Works Association designated the pumphouse a national water landmark. [134]

In 1996 and 1997 the state, using a $7.8 million federal appropriation, lowered, relocated, and beautified the section of the canal for which it was once again responsible. [135] This revitalized portion of the lower central canal has fostered significant new public construction, including the Eiteljorg Museum of American Indians and Western Art, an IMAX theater, the new Indiana State Museum, the headquarters and museum of the National Collegiate Athletic Association (NCAA), and the Congressional Medal of Honor memorial. In 2001, the last manufacturing plant that had been built to run on water power from the downtown portion of the canal was demolished. When the old Beveridge Paper Company building adjacent to the pumphouse fell to the wrecking ball, the final phase of expanding and upgrading the park area began. [136]

Joint efforts among the city, state, and private supporters, along with $70 million of federal funds, have resulted in approximately $400 million of new and renovated development along the banks of the lower canal in downtown Indianapolis. Heading toward its bicentennial in the twenty-first century, the Indiana Central Canal has proved to be (although in different forms from those envisioned by its creators) a priceless asset to the citizens of Indianapolis and central Indiana.

POSTSCRIPT

From 1835 to 1841 official reports of the Central Canal commissioners and engineers to the Indiana legislature indicate that almost 25 miles of the Central Canal were constructed. The canal began in Broad Ripple in Marion County and ran south to the Port Royal bluffs at Waverly on the Johnson/Morgan county line. The thirteen miles of the northern portion of the canal through Marion County were built and permanently watered (from Broad Ripple to Pleasant Run in the southern part of the county).

In contrast, the southern twelve miles of the canal, from Pleasant Run to Waverly, were constructed but never watered. The state ran out of borrowed money and could not finish the southern aqueducts and culverts necessary for creek crossings. According to state legislature reports, the six wooden locks planned for the Johnson County portion of the canal were also never completed. A dam at Waverly, similar to the Broad Ripple dam, was completed, and it remained in use (with water from the White River) until the 1850s.

Johnson County historians Jerry Sargent and Joe McClung have searched for years for remnants of the Central Canal in Johnson County. They have been aided by members of the Canal Society of Indiana, who held caravan tours of the area in 1993 and 1999. These efforts continued while this history was researched and written. Then in December 2001 over one and one-half continuous miles of the 1830s Central Canal were found just north of Waverly.

This southern remnant of the canal has been added to other 20th century rediscoveries of canal remnants and an accurate, center-line route of the Central Canal has been mapped from Broad Ripple all the way to Waverly. The Central Canal has been rediscovered in Johnson County. [137]

View of Canal looking west from State Capitol c. 1935

Courtesy HLFI

J. Darrell Bakken

View of canal looking west from State Office Building, 2001

Courtesy Indianapolis DMD

View of canal looking north from Ohio Street, 1977

Courtesy HLFI

View of canal looking north from Ohio Street, 2001

Courtesy Indianapolis DMD

White River State Park expansion

The old Beveridge Paper Co. building will be razed and transformed into 3½ acres of green space in White River State Park called the Performance Lawn.

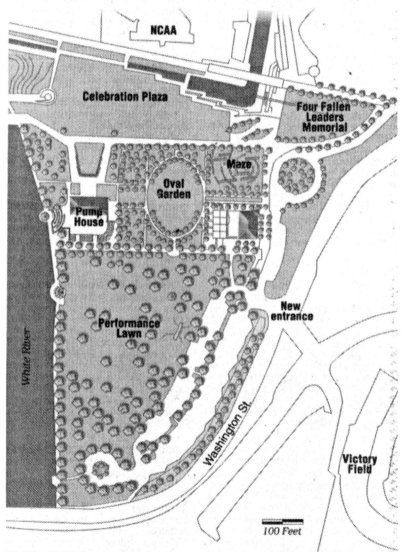

2000 Master Plan for White River State Park
Courtesy Indianapolis <u>Star</u>

The Downtown Canal

Completion of Downtown's 1.3-mile canal will be marked by official dedication of the northern section on Tuesday. City officials say the canal is at the center of $190 million in recent private development and hope the new extension will spur even more development.

Detail

Marion

10th Street Basin

65

11th St.

10th St.

Ninth St.

St. Clair St.

Canal extension

Walnut St.

North St.

Indiana University - Purdue University Indianapolis

Michigan St.

New York St.

Military Park Canal

Ohio St.

White River State Park

Washington St.

Indiana Government Center

Dr. Martin Luther King Jr. St.

Indiana Ave.

West St.

Canal

Senate Ave.

1/8 Mile

Some developments along the canal and their costs:

1 **Indiana Historical Society** $40 million

2 **Canal Square apartments** $25 million

3 **Courtyard by Marriott** $20 million

4 **Canal Overlook apartments** $10.2 million

5 **Historic Landmarks Foundation** $2.1 million

6 **Canal Court apartments** $7.8 million

7 **Indiana University Radiology Associates** $6.9 million

Source: City of Indianapolis

Staff Graphic / Steve Vanderbosch

Map of new developments along downtown canal, May 2001

Courtesy Indianapolis <u>Star</u>

Now That Time Has Had Its Say
A History of the Indianapolis Central Canal, 1835-2002

The proposed widening of U.S. 40 through the historic village of Cumberland—on the eastern edge of Marion County—earned a 10 Most Endangered listing for the entire town back in 1998. Historic Landmarks and Cumberland G.A.P. (Citizens for Smart Growth and Progress) have spent the last three years working with the Indiana Department of Transportation to devise a road widening plan that won't obliterate the area's nineteenth-century architecture.

Historic Landmarks tries to convince county commissioners to retain historic bridges in active use, but we don't always succeed. Even when we fail, the nature of historic iron bridges gives us another chance: the bridges can be dismantled and relocated. Historic Landmarks saved two historic iron bridges from Montgomery County by moving them to Indianapolis, in partnership with Indy Parks and the Indianapolis Museum of Art. Both spans carry pedestrian traffic—the 1872 Bowstring truss bridge at the IMA (above), and the 1869 Bedstead pony truss bridge in Broad Ripple.

FOCUSING ON THE MOST IMPERILED

Historic Landmarks Foundation of Indiana's 10 Most Endangered list shines a spotlight on landmarks in peril. In addition to generating publicity—and positive outcomes—for endangered historic places, we're able to raise awareness of preservation efforts throughout the state. Print, radio and TV media generously cover the 10 Most Endangered, and preservation and neighborhood groups, historical societies, and community development organizations help promote the list. Since the list's inception in 1991, Historic Landmarks has celebrated the saves of 27 Most Endangered entries, compared to only three losses.

Historic Landmarks and the Historic Preservation Association of Jasper County (HPAJC) commissioned feasibility and reuse studies for 10 Most entry Drexel Hall. The studies' recommendations of economically viable reuse options are presently under consideration by the Drexel Hall task force of St. Joseph College. Historic Landmarks has partnered with St. Joseph College and HPAJC to lobby for federal funding for stabilization of the 1888 landmark.

❋ Three of our 10 Most Endangered landmarks for 2000 were moved to saved status: Snow Hill Covered Bridge, Stinesville Main Street, and Long Beach Town Center. Taking their places on the 2001 list, announced in November 2000, are Fairmount High School, the T. C. Steele Boyhood Home in Waveland, and Historic Bridges of Indiana. We've made solid progress in improving the situations of most repeat entries from the list but it would be premature to issue "saved" declarations just yet for Cumberland, Marion County; Drexel Hall, Rensselaer; Gary Union Station; Simpson & Beecher Halls, Indiana School for the Deaf, Indianapolis; Terre Haute House; U.S. Quarter-master Depot, Jeffersonville; Vevay Roller Mill.

❋ For the first time, a thematic listing—historic bridges—appears on our Most Endangered list. Hundreds of Indiana bridges face elimination or replacement. Historic Landmarks' work with Historic

Historic Bridge Relocated to Canal at IMA
Courtesy Historic Landmarks

99

Canal reflects a revitalized Downtown

Staff Photo / Frank Espich

Running the falls: Walkers and joggers couldn't wait for Tuesday's official dedication of the northern extension of the canal. Completion of the 10th Street Basin caps a project begun in 1985.

Basin shimmers as crown jewel in waterway project

By Doug Sword
STAFF WRITER

It is about the same length as the oval track at Indianapolis Motor Speedway, but oh, so much more peaceful.

With completion of the 10th Street Basin, the Downtown Canal is finally finished, giving walkers, joggers and in-line skaters a continuous loop for their exercise and recreation.

Although the northern section of the canal won't be dedicated officially until next week, the 2.6-mile loop was opened several weeks ago as eager canal patrons whisked aside construction barriers in a sort of unofficial dedication of their own.

"That's democracy," chuckled Mayor Bart Peterson, seemingly unconcerned at the stealing of thunder from Tuesday's ceremony, which will feature him and Gov. Frank O'Bannon.

You can hardly blame canal lovers for their enthusiasm. After all, the opening marks an end for the fore-

Dedication planned

Dedication ceremonies for the northern extension of the Downtown Canal will be held from 11 a.m. to 11:30 a.m. Tuesday. The event is open to the public and will be held on the terrace on the west side of the 10th Street Basin. Expected at the ceremony are Mayor Bart Peterson and Gov. Frank O'Bannon.

seeable future of a construction project that started in 1985. While long-term plans envision another unconnected leg of the canal north of I-65, there's no money for it at the moment.

"I like the canal, period," said Max Mieth, who journeyed from his Southside home last weekend to walk along the waterway. "Did you ever see it before this?" he asked, standing in front of the granite waterfall that feeds clear water from a deep well into the basin. "It was a mess; it was a stink."

In place of the marshy canal is a

$33 million waterway connecting White River at the National Institute for Fitness and Sport and the state office complex with a quickly developing corridor stretching north to 11th Street.

City officials estimate that private development worth $190 million has sprouted up within a few blocks of the canal. Development has been minimal along the canal extension north of St. Clair Street that was started in 1999. But that seems destined to change with plans for a biomedical research facility near the 10th Street Basin, housing projects already in the works along the canal's banks and city hopes to turn historic Buggs Temple to the north of the basin into a community-oriented facility.

"It has been one of the most successful urban revitalization programs in the country," said former Mayor Stephen Goldsmith, whose administration began the work on the upper part of the canal.

See CANAL Page 4

Revitalized Canal Encouraged Many New Downtown Projects
Courtesy Indianapolis <u>Star</u>

501 N. Indiana Ave. Canal Side
Courtesy Historic Landmarks

Historic Landmarks of Indiana
New Headquarters Canal Side
Courtesy Historic Landmarks

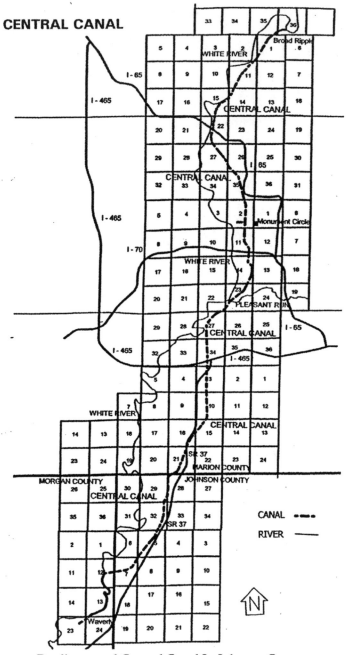

CENTRAL CANAL

Re-discovered Central Canal In Johnson County
Courtesy WTH Engineering

APPENDIX I

1. Lease Agreement between Mill Owner and Indiana Central Canal Company, 1860

An Agreement made this 20th day of March 1860, by and between Henry R. Selden, Nicholas E. Paine and Harmon Woodruff, Trustees of the Indiana Central Company of the first part and James Skillen of the second part.

Whereas a lease has this day been executed by and between the parties hereto, by which the parties of the first part have leased to the party of the second part, for the term of twenty years, water power from the Indiana Central Canal, in the City of Indianapolis, to drive two rums of Mill stones not exceeding however [ ] Cubic feet per minute for each run of stone.

And whereas the number of cubic feet per minute which is to constitute the maximum of such power for each run of stone has been left blank in said lease to be filled hereafter.

Now therefore it is hereby agreed between the said parties, that the said blank shall be filled with the number of cubic feet per minute, which shall be sufficient with sixteen feet head and fall of water, with the use of the best overshot wheel adapted to such head and fall, to furnish the requisite power with the least expenditure of water, and with such millstones and arrangement of other machinery as will require the least expenditure of power for grinding ten bushels per hour of good dry white wheat, and to carry and properly operate such usual and proper machinery as is used or needed in the manufacture of flour such quantity not however to exceed the quantity which may be actually required to do that amount of work by such wheel as may be actually used in case such wheel shall be found to require less water than the best overshot. The quantity within those limits to be determined within 60 days after the mill to be erected by said Skillen in which to use such power shall be erected and in operation by Daniel Marsh, selected by the parties of the first part, and John T. Wilder selected by the party of the second part for that purpose, and in case they shall fail to agree, then the same to be determined within thirty days after the expiration of said sixty days, by an umpire to be selected by them—and when those persons or such umpire shall have presented a certificate fixing such amount, the same shall be inserted in the blank left in said lease for that purpose. In case the said Marsh or said Wilder shall become unable or shall refuse or neglect to act in the matter hereby agreed to be submitted to them then the party naming the one so unable or neglecting may appoint another person, to act in his place, and in default of such appointment, the other of said persons may act alone.

Witness the hands and seals of said parties.

Henry R. Selden
N. E. Paine
H. Woodruff
James Skillen

2. Excerpts from the First Annual Report of the Water Works Company of Indianapolis for the year ending December 31, 1871*

Issue of Stock (p. 4)

The amount of stock issued by the Water Works Company is five hundred thousand dollars, which stock was delivered to the Indiana Central Canal Company as full consideration for the Canal property. This property embraces that part of the Central Canal north of Morgan County, and includes all the real estate purchased and appropriated by the State for the use of the Canal, the right of way, banks, margins, tow-paths, side cuts, feeders, basins, dams, water power, structures, and all the appurtenances thereunto belonging. The chain of title for this property, from the State of Indian to the Water Works Company, is full and complete, and is a matter of public record. The stock issued is full paid stock, and is not subject to further calls.

Expenditures—From Secretary's Report (p. 18)

Real Estate—paid for central canal, etc. $502,668.93

Detailed Abstracts of Expenditures, Statement A—Miscellaneous (p. 19)

Real Estate—paid for central canal	$500,000.00
""—paid lien on canal	20,000.00
""—paid for sundry pieces of ground	2,668.93

List of Real Estate (p. 37)

Conveyed by the Central Canal to the Water Works Company and held by this Company January 1, 1872, with its estimated value.

TOTAL of all items is $150,085.00

*Source: Memorandum by John Kleinhenz, undated, IWC Archives.

3. Notice of lawsuit against Water Works Company of Indianapolis for insufficient water power, 1872

To the Water Works Company of Indianapolis:—

As successor and grantee of the Indiana Central Canal Company you are notified that by the terms of the lease of date of March 20th 1860, from said Company to James Skillen we are entitled to 450 cubic feet of water per minute for each run of stone in our mill, from the Central Canal; that there is now a deficiency of water in said Canal, and we are not having the use of our quantity by at least one half; that by the terms of the lease from said Canal Company to Gay and Braden of May 1st, 1864, it is provided that in case of deficiency of water to supply all the water powers which may be leased or used on the upper level of said Canal, said Gay & Braden were to have the first right to the use of the water to the extent of the power leased to them, subject to the prior right of the said Canal Company, and his assigns, at all times thereafter to have the quantity of water required to supply the power previously leased on the upper level of said Canal, being the power leased by or on account of the State prior to the time of the sale of said Canal by the State, and power leased by said Canal Company to Wiggins & Chandler; to John Carlisle; and to James Skillen, which latter is the lease under which we claim; that the said deficiency of water to supply our mill is caused by the wrongful use and appropriation of the water in said Canal by said Gay & Braden or their assignees, contrary to the terms of their said lease; and we require of you, as grantee of said Canal Company, and because of your assuming the obligations of the said Company, to protect our rights and interests in the premises, and cause said Gay & Braden or their assigns to desist from the use of said water until we receive the amount of water we are entitled to under said lease of March 20th 1860, and in case of your failure to do so we shall hold you responsible to us for all damages sustained, which amounts to the sum of One Hundred dollars per day.

September 4th 1872
Skillen & Sullivan
Pre T. R & S. atty's

4. Excerpt from the Deed for the Sheriff's Sale of the Water Works Company of Indianapolis, April 1881

Sheriff of Marion County to T. Edw. Hambleton et al
April 21, 1881

3893 ½ Sheriff Marion CountyTo T. E. Hambleton et al.

This indenture made this 21st day of April A. D. 1881 between Henry C. Adams Sheriff of Marion County in the State of Indiana of the first part and T. Edward Hambleton and John M. Denison of the City of Baltimore in the State of Maryland and E. Delaven Woodruff of the City of Auburn in the State of New York as Trustee as hereinafter mentioned parties of the second part.

Whereas at the March Term A. D. 1881 of the Superior Court of Marion County in the State of Indiana and on the twelfth day of March of said year William Henderson Trustee as the Plaintiff in a certain foreclosure suit then pending in said Court wherein the Water Works Company of Indianapolis Indiana and others were defendants recovered a Judgment or decree of foreclosure for the sum of One Million One hundred and Thirty Thousand one hundred and fifty six dollars and ten cents ($1,130,156.10) and costs taxed at the sum of Five Hundred and fifty one dollars and fifty cents ($551.50) which decree embodied an order of sale for the sale of the property therein described and directed to be sold for the satisfaction of said decree interest and costs as will more fully appear by said decree now of record in said Court reference being thereunto had.

And whereas afterwards on the 25th day of March A. D. 1881 a copy of said Judgment or decree of foreclosure and order of sale was duly issued by the Clerk of said Court under the seal of said Court and directed and delivered by said Clerk said Henry C. Adams and Sheriff of said County to be executed.

.... And whereas the said Water Works property as sold to the said parties of the second part as trustees as aforesaid is described in the said decree of foreclosure and order of sale and in said certified copy thereof as well as in the notices of sale so given by said Sheriff as aforesaid as follows towit;

The following described Water Works property of the Water Works Company of Indianapolis Indiana with all and singular the appurtenances thereunto belonging embracing that part of the Central Canal which is situated in the County of Marion and the State of Indiana and which lies north of the line of Morgan County in said State (except as hereinafter excepted) including its banks margins to[w] paths said cuts feeders basins right of way dams waterpowers structures and all the leases of water power and of lands and tenements and right to cut Ice and any other leases or contracts relating to any parts of said Canal property to which the said Water Works Company is entitled being and intended to be all the property and rights now held by said Water Works Company conveyed to said Company by the Indiana Central Canal Company by Deed dated May 1, 1870, (except as hereinafter excepted) also all the rights privileges and corporate franchises of the said Water Works Company as a Water Works Corporation under and by virtue of the laws of Indiana and the ordinances of the Common Council of said City of Indianapolis also all the property of every name character kind or description including lands buildings machinery tools water pipes mains fire hydrants and fixtures owned or that have been constructed for or in any way acquired or owned by said Water Works Company, connected with or arising out of or appertaining to its business of furnishing said City of Indianapolis and the inhabitants thereof with water also all water rents and all revenues derived or to be derived therefrom or from any other sources or growing out of any losses or contracts heretofore made and still existing excepting however from such sale so much of the main line of said Canal as is situate south of south line of Market Street in said City of Indianapolis and which was conveyed by said Water Works Company to the Indianapolis Cincinnati and Lafayette Rail Road Company by Deed dated the third day of September A. D. 1873 and recorded in the Recorders Office of Marion County aforesaid in Town Lot Record No 77 at page 380 and following pages. The said Water Works property so to be sold embraces the following parcels of Real Estate situated in said County of Marion to-wit:

[Eleven parcels of Central Canal, Washington Station, and Broad Ripple Dam land are subsequently listed in legal land description language, to complete all of the Central Canal land transfer from WWCI to IWC.]

J. Darrell Bakken

APPENDIX II

CANAL INDUSTRIAL WATER USE CUSTOMERS

1839 to 1870

Aldrich & Gay Lumber Yard, Michigan Street and Indiana Avenue

American Brewing Company, 352-53 West Ohio Street

Blake & Gentle's Planing Mill

Myron Brown & Company, flour mill

Brower & Love Cotton Mill, New York Street and Blake Street

Buncom & Springer Box Factory and Veneer Mill, canal at St. Clair Street

Burke & Morris sawmill and flour mill, Broad Ripple

Caledonia Paper Mill, Market Street and South Basin

Carlisle Flour Mill, Washington Street and Geisendorff Street

Chandler & Taylor Plant, west of Carlisle

Eaglesfield Sawmill, adjacent to site of Washington Station

Cornelius Free (flour mill, carding mill, and sawmill), Port Royal, Waverly

Flour Mill, Missouri Street and Market Street lock

Geisendorff Woolen Factory, National Road and Washington Street

Gibson Mill, 352-54 West Washington Street

Holt Ice & Storage, Missouri Street and Walnut Street

Indianapolis Bleaching Company, north of Brower & Love

Indianapolis Chair Manufacturing, canal between Vermont Street and New York Street

Indianapolis Cotton, National Road and Blake Street

Indianapolis Excelsior Manufacturing, canal flume north of Market Street

Indianapolis Gas Company, Pratt Street and Market Street

Indianapolis Rolling Mill, Merrill Street and Tennessee Street

Johnson Danley & Company, 336-80 West Market Street

Kingan & Company Packing House, river at foot of Maryland

Street

Koontz & Burke Sawmill, Broad Ripple

McCarty Hemp Factory, Ray Street and Tennessee Street

Mack's Carpet & Rug Factory, canal and Cora Street

Merritt & Coughlin's Woolen Mill, replaced Scudder and Hannerman mill

Protzman Soap Factory, canal and McCarty Street

Ogden Sawmill

Sandstrom Short-Turn Buggy Company, replaced Merritt & Coughlin's mill

Scudder & Hannerman Oil and Cotton Mill, canal flume at foot of Washington Street

Udell Woodenware Works, 27th Street and Udell Street

Underhill Gristmill, Bluff Street and Wisconsin Street

Vinton Paper Mill, replaced Eaglesfield Sawmill

W. G. Wasson & Company Lumberyard, east of canal, Michigan Street and Walnut Street

West's Cotton Mill, on canal near Fall Creek

Yandes & Sheets Paper Mill, Missouri Street and Market Street lock

Source: Harlan, "Central in the City," appendix III, 1-5.

1910

Acme Milling Company

American Brewing Company

Artificial Ice & Cold Storage Company

Balke & Krauss Company

Beveridge Paper Company

Brower & Love Cotton Mill

City Ice Company

Dean Brothers Steam Pump Works

Excelsior Mill Property

Holt Ice & Cold Storage Company

W. D. Huffman
Indianapolis Light & Heat Company
Frank Janes
Kingan & Company, Ltd., Packing House
Oscar Klugel
Laycock Power House
Merchants Heat and Light Company
Mooney Land
Riverside Bathing Beach Company
Woolen Mill Property

Sources: Leonard Metcalf and John W. Alvord, "Indianapolis Water Co. Canal Data," May 1910 report, 142 (IWC Archives).

1945

Beveridge Paper Company, adjacent to Washington Station
Capital Ice Company, 356 W. North Street [contract cancelled November 1945]
Dean Brothers Pump Company, 323 W. 10th Street, east side of canal
Indianapolis Power & Light Company, Mill Street Station
Indianapolis Power & Light Company, Perry West Station
Kingan Packing Company, south of Washington Station

Source: Memorandum from Claris Allen, December 5, 1945, Drawer #119, Engineering Department Files (IWC Archives)

J. Darrell Bakken

APPENDIX III

CANAL OWNERS

1839-1851	State of Indiana
1851-1864	Indiana Central Canal Manufacturing, Hydraulic, and Water Works Company, Rochester, New York
1864-1870	Indiana Central Canal Company, Rochester, New York
1870-1881	Water Works Company of Indianapolis, Indianapolis
1881—	Indianapolis Water Company

CANAL HISTORY TIME LINE

1835	The 290-mile center-line survey is completed from the Wabash River to the Ohio River
January 27, 1836	Governor Noah Noble signs the Internal Improvements Act of 1836
October 1836	Contractor John Burke begins construction of Broad Ripple dam and canal
1838	Canal commissioners run out of construction funds; work stopped at Pleasant Run
June 27, 1839	The 13-mile watered and operational Central Canal is placed in service from the Broad Ripple dam and headgates to the outlet structure at Pleasant Run Creek; contractors have been paid $434,716 to date
1840s	Severe canal maintenance problems for the state of Indiana

115

June 30, 1851	Canal is deeded to Central Canal Manufacturing, Hydraulic and Water Works Company of Rochester, New York, for $2,425
March 11, 1864	Canal is deeded to the Indiana Central Canal Company of Rochester, New York
October 7, 1869	Articles of Association of the private Water Works Company of Indianapolis
December 28, 1870	Canal deeded to WWCI
June 1, 1871	WWCI begins public water utility operations, including canal water turbines for pumping into the system
April 21, 1881	Marion County Sheriff sells assets and customers of bankrupt WWCI to newly formed private Indianapolis Water Company
1889	Fairview Park and associated streetcar line from downtown Indianapolis create first major recreational uses of canal
1904	Canal is used to convey White River surface water supply from Broad Ripple to White River Treatment Plant, for a major savings in inlet pumping costs
1904	Major flood destroys canal aqueduct over Fall Creek, rebuilt in 1905
1909	Alvord & Metcalf report on the financial value of the canal
1910	High bridge at West 29th Street is removed, ending use of boats on the canal
1912	Clarence H. Geist of Philadelphia buys IWC
March 1913	Record flood of White River causes the first major breach of the canal, extensive damage of various structures from Broad

116

	Ripple south, and cutoff of city water supply for several days
1923	Metcalf engineering study recommends major upgrades; canal valuation is included in IWC utility rate base for the first time
Spring 1926	First canal bank slippage in the Highbanks area east of Michigan Road
November 1926	*McCardle* v. *Indianapolis Water Company*, the first U.S. Supreme Court case involving IWC and the canal
1927	Front of Washington Station blown off in a tornado
May 1938	*McCart* v. *Indianapolis Water Company*, second U.S. Supreme Court case involving the canal
1952	IWC sold to Murchison family of Dallas, Texas
1955	Last high bridge over the canal at Butler University is retired
1963	Major bank slippage at Highbanks
1969	Washington Station and canal water pumping turbines are retired from service
April 1971	Canal at Indianapolis Museum of Art is designated an AWWA Water Landmark
1972	IWC donates 2.25 miles of the canal through downtown to trust on behalf of city
September 1975	Waterways Task Force prepares "The Lower Central Canal" report for Historic Landmarks Foundation
1976	City of Indianapolis takes title to 2.25 miles of the downtown canal
October 1980	City deeds lower one-half mile of canal (central mill race) to state of Indiana

April 21, 1982	City Metropolitan Development Commission approves Northwest Redevelopment Project urban renewal plan
November 12, 1982	Washington Street Pumping Station is designated an AWWA Water Landmark
July 1986	First construction contract for the Canal Walk redevelopment project
February 1996	Revised Canal Walk design guidelines are issued
1996—1997	Canal from West Street Bridge to White River State Park is relocated, lowered, and beautified as site for three new museums and renovated Washington Pumphouse
2000—2001	Beveridge Paper Company, last remaining commercial user of canal water, purchased by White River State Park and demolished
May 29, 2001	Dedication ceremony for final project of Canal Walk

PHOTOGRAPH CREDITS

Butler University Archives: 72 top

Canal Society of Indiana (CSI): x

Rita W. Harlan: 27

Historic Landmarks Foundation of Indiana (HLFI): Cover, 49 bottom,
75 bottom, 93, 95,
99, 101

Chuck Huppert: xi

O. James Fox and Indiana Historical Society (IHS): iv, 76, 22, 47, 73 top

Indiana State Library: 21, 24 top, 25, 30, 31

Indianapolis Department of Metropolitan Development (DMD): 94,
96

Indianapolis Museum of Art (IMA): 81

Indianapolis <u>Star</u> and <u>News:</u> 48 top, 75 top, 77, 78, 97, 98, 100

Indianapolis Water Company (IWC): v, 26, 28-29, 43, 44-45, 46, 47, 48
bottom, 49, 50, 51, 52, 68, 69, 70, 71, 72,
73, 74, 80, 82

Tippecanoe County Historical Society: 24 bottom

WTH Engineering: xii, 102

[1] The history of the 25-mile portion of the Central Canal built in Marion and Johnson counties is described in Paul Fatout, *Indiana Canals* (West Lafayette, Ind., 1972), quotation pp. 72–73; Rita W. Harlan, "The Central in the City: The Impact of the Central Canal in Indianapolis, 1836–1900," (M.A. thesis, 1996, Indiana University–Purdue University at Indianapolis); and the *Indiana House Journal* from 1835 through 1841. A contemporary account of the Internal Improvements Act can be found in the Indianapolis *Journal*, January 19, 1836.

[2] Fatout, *Indiana Canals*, 76-77.

[3] Typescript of IWC document, "Canal" file, c. 1910, DMD Historic Preservation Archives, Indianapolis.

[4] Indianapolis *Journal*, May 31, 1871.

[5] Larry Coffey and Paula Whitney, Indianapolis, Department of Metropolitan Development, interview with author April 10, 2001.

[6] On the transition from territory to state, see Donald F. Carmony, *Indiana, 1816-1850: The Pioneer Era*, Vol. II, *The History of Indiana* (Indianapolis, 1998). In 1821 the junction of White River and Fall Creek occurred at what is today West Washington Street; the junction was moved north to West 10th Street in 1874.

[7] Carmony, *Indiana*, 111.

[8] *Ibid.*, 145.

[9] Fatout, *Indiana Canals*, 52.

[10] "Calvin Fletcher at Two Hundred: 1798-1998," *Traces of Indiana and Midwestern History*, X (Winter 1998), 34.

[11] For the text of the Internal Improvements Act, see *Laws of Indiana*, Twentieth Session, 1835-1836, 6-10. Port Royal is today the town of Waverly.

[12] 1835 State Legislature Report, 67.

[13] "The Central Canal, an interview with Gen. T. A. Morris, engineer in 1898," *Indiana Magazine of History* III (September 1907), 115–16 (hereafter cited as "Central Canal interview").

[14] Harlan, "Central in the City".

[15] The community of Broad Ripple was surveyed, laid out, and platted as forty-eight lots on the north side of the canal by Jacob C. Coil on April 20, 1837. The community of Wellington was platted on the canal's south side as thirty-two lots by James A. and Adam R. Nelson on May 17, 1837. Berry R. Sulgrove, *History of Indianapolis and Marion County, Indiana* (Philadelphia, 1884; reprint, Evansville, Ind., 1974), 637.

[16] 1837 State Legislature Report. State ownership of the land later became important in legal proceedings concerning ownership and valuation of the canal.

[17] Steve Savage, Broad Ripple: A Rough River Town to a Suburb of Indianapolis (Indianapolis, 1965), 3.

[18] Patrick J. Furlong, *Indiana: An Illustrated History* (Northridge, Calif., 1985), 62; Junior History Society of Broad Ripple High School, *The History of Broad Ripple* (Indianapolis, 1968), 7.

[19] Typescript , c. 1910, "Canal" File, (Department of Metropolitan Development Preservation Archives, Indianapolis.)

[20] There were, in fact, two locks in addition to the stone lock; the mill referred to was Underhill Mill. See Harlan, "Central in the City," appendix III, 4.

[21] The other primary use of the canal at the time was roundtrip pleasure rides via excursion boat from Broad Ripple to Indianapolis.

[22] 1838 State Legislature Reports, 117; 1839 State Legislature Reports, 90–91.

[23] Fatout estimates the speed of a packet boat pulled by three horses or mules at four to eight miles per hour; larger freight boats carrying several tons of goods would have gone no faster than two miles per hour. Fatout, *Indiana Canals*, 133.

[24] Robert C. Earle, typescript of speech "The Indiana Central Canal," American Water Works Association American Water Landmark Dedication, Indianapolis, Ind., August 11, 1971 (copy in IWC Archives).

[25] Later development in this area included Woodstock Country Club, the International Center, Christian Theological Seminary, and Butler University.

[26] Kate Milner Rabb, "A Hoosier Listening Post," Indianapolis *Star*, February 4, 5, 6, 1926. This three-part newspaper series quotes 1874 remembrances found in the scrapbook of the late Luther Short of Franklin, Ind. The columns contain a great deal of early Central Canal history, especially from 1836 to 1840. Among many topics that Short recalled were the opening day ceremonies for the canal on June 27, 1839, and some of the mills that were built along the canal.

[27] Annual payments for water power were the major source of revenue, but boat tolls also provided some income. "Regarding the Central Canal Chain to Title, etc.," File #154, Finance and Accounting Files (IWC Archives).

[28] Deed abstract, Indiana Title Guaranty & Loan Company, 1881, p. 3 (IWC Archives), hereafter cited as Deed Abstract 1881. The sale price for the June 1851 deed was $2,425; see Fatout, *Indiana Canals*, 143.

[29] Deed Abstract 1881, 3.

[30] See *Laws of Indiana*, 1851, "An act to incorporate the Central Canal Manufacturing, Hydraulic, and Water Works Company," 358-60.

[31] 1839 State Legislature Report, 90. The construction cost is for the completed canal (24 miles, 58 chains) from Broad Ripple to Port Royal.

[32] "Central Canal interview," 115–16.

[33] Indianapolis *Journal*, November 15, 1851.

[34] Indianapolis *Journal*, April 15, 1857.

[35] See Appendix II on mills along the canal. Using information from existing canal histories, I have approximated total lease payments based on the number of mills and the maximum annual payments.

[36] Indianapolis *Journal*, November 16, 1858.

[37] Deed Abstract 1881, 7.

[38] Indianapolis *Journal*, March 24, December 2, 1859.

[39] Indianapolis *Journal*, February 29, 1860.

[40] Assumed to be about West 38th Street and the canal, where White River and the canal are adjacent.

[41] Jacob P. Dunn, *Greater Indianapolis: The History, the Industries, the Institutions and the People of a City of Homes*, 2 vols. (Chicago, 1910), 30–31.

[42] Indianapolis *Journal*, March 3, 1860.

[43] Dunn, *Greater Indianapolis*, 332. These histories do not mention the suggested water supply source.

[44] "History of the Water Supply of Indianapolis," p. 12. Catherwood & Company would later be involved in competition for the city natural gas contract and the street railway project.

[45] Dunn, *Greater Indianapolis*, 331.

[46] A Holly steam pump is a four-cylinder condensing steam-pump engine with four steam cylinders and four pumps.

[47] "History of the Water Supply of Indianapolis," 12–13.

[48] Deed Abstract 1881, 7.

[49] These are the names found in two sources: "History of the Water Supply of Indianapolis," 15, and Dunn, *Greater Indianapolis*, 332. Giffin, *Water Runs Downhill*, 18, also lists Aquilla Jones as an original director and William Wallace as an original subscriber. W. R. Holloway includes William Henderson and Deloss Root of Indiana, as well as Harmon Woodruff and Henry B. Selden of Rochester, New York, as directors; Holloway, *Indianapolis: A Historical and Statistical Sketch of the Railroad City* (Indianapolis, 1870), 281.

[50] See a full transcript of the franchise in the Indianapolis *Journal*, November 20, 1869.

[51] Dunn, *Greater Indianapolis*, 332; the franchise was amended January 3 and 24 of the same year.

[52] In March 1923 the state Public Service Commission granted Indianapolis Water Company, the owner of the canal, an indeterminate permit; see Public Service Commission of Indiana Order #6996, March 30, 1923 (IWC Archives).

[53] The deed lists Harmon Woodruff, president, and Edward H. Avery, secretary, for the Indiana Central Canal Company and James O. Woodruff as president of the Water Works Company of Indianapolis. Holloway, *Indianapolis*, 281.

[54] Robert C. Earle speech, undated memorandum of John E. Kleinhenz (IWC archives).

[55] See Appendix I.

[56] Indianapolis *Journal*, May 31, 1871; Holloway, *Indianapolis*, records the cost of the initial work as $350,000, p. 281.

[57] Dunn, *Greater Indianapolis*, 332; Giffin, *Water Runs Downhill*, 19.

[58] Thurman B. Rice, *The Hoosier Health Officer: A Biography of Dr. J. N. Hurty and The History of the Indiana State Board of Health to 1925* (N.P., 1947), 30.

[59] Dunn, *Greater Indianapolis*, 332. In this chapter the figures for households assume five persons per household.

[60] *Ibid.*

[61] Giffin, *Water Runs Downhill*, 20.

[62] Harlan, "Central in the City," Appendix III, p. 2.

[63] Deed Abstract 1881, 16.

[64] Harlan, "Central in the City," 4–5.

[65] "Survey by Joseph H. Dennis, deputy Marion County surveyor, as certified by Harvey B. Fatout, county surveyor, on June 30, 1877," Drawing Files, Engineering Department (IWC Archives).

[66] Deed Record for Indiana Central Canal, Sheriff of Marion County to T. Edw. Hambleton et al., Apr. 21, 1881, File 1528 (IWC Archives), hereafter cited as Deed Record of 1881.

[67] Deed Abstract 1881, 9–10.

[68] The sum is calculated based on an 1880 city population of 75,000, estimating five persons per residential household.

[69] Deed Record of 1881.

[70] Revenues continued to be low until they ceased altogether after 1910, when most of the high- clearance bridges that had permitted canal navigation began to be replaced by low-clearance bridges.

[71] Davis was a member of the Indiana Banking Company and acted as treasurer to help protect the bank's loans to the IWC. He organized company finances but also often took it upon himself to supervise construction projects. He became IWC's vice-president in 1885 and served as company president from 1904 to 1909. Giffin, *Water Runs Downhill*, 28, 45–55.

[72] The first IWC directors were John M. Denison, Albert (Abram) W. Hendricks, Oscar B. Hord, Conrad Baker, Albert Baker, E. Delevan Woodruff, John C. New, Ingram Fletcher, and Christopher Heckman. *Ibid.*, 26–29.

[73] Morris remained president of IWC until his death in 1904 at age 93. In the 1830s he had been in charge of completing the national road from Richmond to Indianapolis and had been the engineer in charge of surveying and inspecting construction of the Central Canal. By the 1840s he had become a major figure in the state's railroads and continued to be during and after the Civil War. *Ibid.*, 30–43.

[74] In 1909 Dr. John N. Hurty, M.D., became one of the founders of the Indiana Section of the American Water Works Association and was the state's most eminent public health officer during the early years of the state Board of Health.

[75] Indianapolis News, August 1, 2, 1881; J. N. Hurty, "History of Indiana's Water Supply," in Conference of Municipal and Private Owned Water Plants of Indiana with the State Board of Health at Indianapolis, July 8 and 9, 1908 (Indianapolis, 1908), 12. On Hurty and his career in public health, see Jeff Bennett and Richard D. Feldman, "'The Most Useful Citizen of Indiana': John N. Hurty and the Public Health Movement," *Traces of Indiana and Midwestern History*, XII (Summer 2000), 34–43.

[76] "History of the Water Supply of Indianapolis," 30.

[77] Indianapolis Water Company, Annual Statistical Data Sheet, 1904–1994 (IWC Archives), hereafter cited as IWC Annual Statistical Data Sheet. A population of 105,000 assumes 21,000 potential residential customers, at five persons per household.

[78] The canal broadcut was a section of the canal, just south of the Fall Creek aqueduct, constructed much wider than the rest of the canal. It allowed the north- and south-bound canal boats to more easily pass each other.

[79] The filter process is explained in "History of the Water Supply of Indianapolis," 37. See also Harry E. Jordan, "Development of Water Treatment at Indianapolis," *Engineering News Record* (reprint; November 10, 1927).

[80] Joseph H. Dennis, engineer, to F. A. W. Davis, November 21, 1902 (IWC Archives).

[81] Walter B. Hendrickson, *The Indiana Years, 1903–1941* Indiana Historical Society Publications, XXVI (Indianapolis, 1983), 85–87.

[82] David G. Vanderstel and Connie Zeigler, *In Pursuit of Leisure Time: The Development and Role of Amusement Parks in Indianapolis, 1880–1970* (Indianapolis, 1992), 27–34.

[83] John E. Kleinhenz, undated memorandum re: Recreational Uses of Canal (IWC Archives).

[84] *Ibid.*; Historic Landmarks Foundation of Indiana, *The Lower Central Canal: A Preservation Program* (Indianapolis, 1975), 18.

[85] Indianapolis *News*, June 24, 1907.

[86] Davis served as IWC president until his death in 1909. Boyd, president of Manufacturers Natural Gas (MNG) of Indianapolis, became a board member in 1901, IWC vice-president in 1904, and president from 1909 to 1912. Landon, an MNG officer from 1892 to 1902 and Davis's son-in-law, became IWC secretary in 1902 and served as vice-president from 1909 to 1912.

[87] IWC sold its portion of the land to Indianapolis contractor Huber, Hunt and Nichols for excavation of Interstate Highway 65 fill, with the proviso that when excavation was complete, the remaining land and newly excavated lake would be donated to the art museum. Giffin, *Water Runs Downhill*, 62; "Deed Agreement Respecting Real Estate," Indianapolis Water Company and Huber, Hunt & Nichols, September 11, 1968 (IWC Archives); "Pledge of Gift From Huber, Hunt & Nichols, Inc. to Art Association of Indianapolis, Indiana," September 11, 1968 (IWC Archives).

[88] The first two aqueducts of 1838 and 1870 were made of wood. The third, built in 1882, was constructed of iron and wood. The fourth steel structure was installed by Massilon Bridge Company of Ohio in 1890. "Annual Report," Indianapolis Water Company, 1953, p. 13, Public Relations Department Files (IWC Archives).

[89] See Appendix II for a list of the companies that used canal water and their payments to IWC in 1909.

[90] This canal valuation would become a part of IWC's water rates in 1923.

[91] For exact figures, see John V. Alvord and Leonard Metcalf, "Report Upon the Reproduction Cost of the Property of the IWC as of Date March 31, 1909," May 1910, Files of the Secretary (IWC Archives). The high valuation of the canal and its importance for the total valuation of the company proved significant in later years for water rate increase cases and related court cases.

[92] "Mill Street Station" File, Engineering Department Files (IWC Archives).

[93] Butler *Collegian*, March 5, 1929, June 4, 1930. According to the Butler newspaper the Native Americans were Mohawk from Ithaca, New York; Hendrickson recalls they were Ojibwa from Wisconsin. See Hendrickson, *The Indiana Years*, 87–88. The pageant was probably also produced earlier, at least in the summers of 1908 and 1909; see "The Canal Book of Ernest Melick [IWC Canal patrolman]," May 30, 1908 to February 28,

1910, File 518, pp. 8, 92 (IWC Archives), in which Melick mentions use permits for the pageant in those years.

[94] Geist relinquished the presidency under a new Public Utility law requiring that all officers and a board majority of any public utility had to be Indiana residents. The law was amended in 1917. When Geist resumed the office of president, Kirk became general manager of IWC and served in that capacity until 1923, when he left to become a vice-president of Citizens Gas Company. Carlton E. Davis succeeded Kirk as company manager; Howard S. Morse took over the job in 1925. See Giffin, *Water Runs Downhill*, 90–91, 97, 121.

[95] To follow the history of the flood of 1913, see the Indianapolis *News*, March 24–29, 31, 1913.

[96] Giffin, *Water Runs Downhill*, 97–100.

[97] "Judicial and Legislative History of the Central Canal," Files of the Secretary (IWC Archives).

[98] *McCardle v. Indianapolis Water Company*, 47 S. Ct. 144 (1923).

[99] Canal Highbanks File, Engineering Department Files (IWC Archives).

[100] Indianapolis *Star*, October 22, 1932.

[101] *McCart v. Indianapolis Water Company*, 89 Fed. 2d, 522 (7th Cir.) 1937.

[102] The 1940 U.S. census showed the population of Indianapolis as 386,972; Marion County's was 460,926. IWC's estimated service population was 401,000. "Statistical Abstract of Indianapolis and Marion County," in *Encyclopedia of Indianapolis*, eds. David J. Bodenhamer and Robert G. Barrows (Bloomington, Ind., 1994), 1506; IWC Statistical Data, Engineering Department, 1904–1994 (IWC Archives).

[103] See Appendix II for lists of the canal's industrial water-use customers from 1839 to 1870, in 1910, and in 1944. Engineering Department Memo, June 23, 1944 (IWC Archives).

[104] Indianapolis Power & Light Co.'s Mill Street Station Canal Water Contract, IWC Memorandum, February 28, 1946 (IWC Archives). As an example, the monthly bill for the Mill Street Station in October 1942 was $264.27. IPL and IWC also had a canal water contract for the Perry "W" plant downtown, near the canal forebay and Washington Station.

[105] O. James Fox, *Gone But Not Forgotten* (Indianapolis, Ind., 2000) 3, 23; Giffin, *Water Runs Downhill*, 155–57.

[106] The third official survey of the canal was performed by civil engineer P. I. Cripe in 1947 and 1948; see "Canal Surveys File," Engineering Department Files (IWC Archives). In 1950 the census population of Marion County was 551,777, and the city's was 427,173. IWC's estimated service population was 480,000. In 1960 IWC's service population was 575,000 and water consumption was 68 million gallons per day(mgd); the population of Indianapolis was 476,258, and Marion County's was 697,567. In 1970 IWC's service population was 680,000 and consumption reached 92.6 mgd; total Uni-Gov/Marion County population was 792,299. By this time IWC had expanded its water service into adjacent Hamilton and Hendricks counties. "Statistical Abstract," *Encyclopedia of Indianapolis*, 1506; IWC Statistical Data, 1904–1994 (IWC Archives).

[107] When the Murchisons bought IWC, they brought Howard S. Morse out of retirement to assume the company presidency in January 1953. Morse became chairman of the board in 1956. Thomas W. Moses, who came from Dallas to Indianapolis to represent the Murchisons at the company, replaced Morse as president in 1956 and became chairman in 1961. One year later Jack Reich became the company's CEO and served in that office until 1967. IWC's current headquarters was built after the Murchisons acquired the company.

[108] Morse Reservoir, completed in 1956, was named after then-chairman Howard S. Morse.

[109] Butler *Collegian*, September 27, 1955.

[110] Indianapolis *Times*, May 12, 1958.

[111] 1835 State Legislature Report, 45. The first high bluff was at the High Banks, the second at what is now Stop 11 Road and Belmont Street in southern Marion County, and the third was the Royal Bluffs at Waverly on the Johnson-Morgan county line.

[112] G. A. Leonards and J. R. Hooper, "Final Report on Investigation of Embankment Instabilities, Indianapolis Water Company High Banks Canal," May 15, 1968 (IWC Archives). One recommendation of the report, lining the canal bottom with plastic sheeting, quickly became counterproductive and was abandoned.

[113] Jack Reich to Mass Transportation Authority, County Metropolitan Planning Commission, May 1, 1967 (IWC Archives); Indianapolis *Star*, August 27, 1967; Indianapolis *News*, April 8, July 29, 1968.

[114] During the mid-1960s IWC was also negotiating with the city to purchase water from the proposed Eagle Creek reservoir. A contract was executed in 1968, and a new 19.2-mgd Eagle Creek water treatment plant and high-lift pumping station went into service in 1976.

[115] Thomas W. Moses to John Walls, February 9, 1970 (IWC Archives). In 1967 IWC's Chief Executive Officer (CEO) Jack Reich resigned, and President Dan Morse retired. Roy Echols became chairman, and Ralph Swingley retired. In its dealings with the City of Indianapolis from 1970 Thomas Moses returned as CEO when Echols and Swingley retired. In its dealings with the City of Indianapolis from 1970 on, the company was working with a new system of city-county metropolitan government called Uni-Gov, which encompassed both Indianapolis and Marion County as a whole.

[116] Richard G. Lugar to Thomas W. Moses, January 15, 1971; Thomas W. Moses to Indiana National Bank Trust Department, 1972; Thomas W. Moses to Indiana National Bank Trust Department, 1973; and William H. Hudnut, III, to Thomas W. Moses, November 24, 1976 (IWC Archives). See also Warranty Deed of March 6, 1972, and Corrective Instrument and Deed of April 25, 1973, Files of the Secretary (IWC Archives).

[117] By 1980 water consumption by IWC's service population had reached 98.53 million gallons per day (mgd). The company was serving a population of 703,500 (compared with the Uni-Gov population of 765,223). Water service now extended beyond the county line into Hancock County. IWC underwent three changes in leadership from the 1970s through the 1990s: Thomas Moses was chief executive officer and president

from 1970 to 1976 and chairman until 1986; Robert McConnell was company chair from 1986 to 1991; James Morris became chair in 1991.

[118] "Canal Barge Idea Springs Major Leak," Indianapolis *News*, December 21, 1982.

[119] William Meyer, "Geohydrologic Setting of and Seepage from a Water-Supply Canal, (Indianapolis, November 1979); Black & Veatch Engineers and Architects, "Evaluation of Surface Water Supply for Indianapolis Water Company," March 1985 (IWC Archives); IWC Annual Statistical Data Sheet. By 1990 water consumption by IWC's service population was nearly 117 mgd, and the company served an estimated population of 753,000. Water service now extended into Boone County as well.

[120] James W. Shaffer, "Triumph Out of Chaos," Indianapolis Water Company publication, July 1992 (IWC Archives).

[121] Service additions included Eastern Morgan Rural Water in Morgan County, the city of Lawrence in Marion County, the towns of McCordsville and New Palestine in Hancock County, and Darlington Water Company in Montgomery County.

[122] This estimate is based on annual average-day canal flows of 75 mgd and electricity costs of 5 cents per kilowatt-hour for pumping. By contrast, in 1905, when flow through the canal approximated 20 mgd and electricity cost 1 cent per kilowatt-hour, the canal saved the utility about $20,000.

[123] The term Central Canal is used again because ownership of three tracts returned to the original owner, the state government.

[124] IWC Canal Land Trust to Indiana National Bank, 1972 and 1973 (IWC Archives); William H. Hudnut, III, to Thomas W. Moses, November 24, December 27, 1976 (IWC Archives).

[125] Members of the Waterways Task Force were James E. Dora, chair and president, General Hotels Corporation; Michael A. Carroll, deputy mayor of Indianapolis; George S. Diener, chair, Indiana State Office Building Commission; Harold J. Egenes, director, Indianapolis Department of Metropolitan Development (DMD); George K. Erganian, president, Henry B. Steeg & Associates, Inc.; Sue Ann Gilroy, director, Indianapolis Department of Parks and Recreation; Dr. Glenn W. Irwin, Jr., vice-president IUPUI; Robert N. Kennedy, partner, Kennedy, Brown & Trueblood; John L. Krauss, executive director, Greater Indianapolis Progress Committee; William L. Leiber, president, Leiber Equipment Company; Ewing Miller, president, Archonics Corporation; Lawrence R. O'Conner, associate, Woollen Associates; Ted Pantazis, director, Governor's Office of Planning & Research; Harold W. Rominger, head, DMD Urban Design Division; Maurice C Stout, vice-president, IWC; William Latz, executive director, Indiana State Office Building Commision; Fred L. Madorin, director, Indianapolis Department of Transportation; Dr. Edward C. Moore, executive vice-chancellor, IUPUI; Hon. Robert D. Orr, lieutenant governor of Indiana; Frank Reed, Jr., president, Midtown Economic Development & Industrial Corporation; William I. Spencer, director, Indianapolis Department of Public Works; and J Reid Williamson, Jr., executive director, Historic Landmarks Foundation of Indiana.

[126] A Lilly Endowment grant to the city's Department of Parks and Recreation funded the study,which was conducted by a San Antonio, Texas firm; see Graves, Fernandez,

Barry, Telford and Associates, Inc., "Indianapolis Waterways Feasibility Study," July 1974.

[127] J. Reid Williamson, Jr. supervised the study, with assistance from the city's DMD, the Greater Indianapolis Progress Committee, the Midtown Economic Development & Industrial Corporation, IUPUI, Evans Woollen Associates, the Indiana State Office Building Commission, and Archonics Corporation, all members of the Waterways Task Force.

[128] Historic Landmarks Foundation of Indiana, *The Lower Central Canal: A Preservation Program* (Indianapolis, 1975).

[129] Indianapolis Metropolitan Development Commission Resolutions of March 17 and April 21, 1982 (DMD Archives, City–County Building, Indianapolis).

[130] Browning, Day, Mullins and Dierdorf Architects, Wetzel Engineers, and Ratio Architects were the prime design and coordinating consultants to DMD.

[131] The work follows design guidelines prepared by Ratio Architects in February 1996. The final plans and specifications for the last phase were prepared by Sasaki Design Team for the U.S. Army Corps of Engineers, Louisville District.

[132] Canal Walk planning and construction took place under four different mayors—Lugar, Hudnut, Goldsmith, and Peterson. DMD directors during this period were Harold Egenes, Robert Kennedy, John Krauss, David Carley, Mike Higbee, Daniel Kazlowski, Elaine Bedel, Moira Carlstedt, Eugene Lausch, and Carolyn Coleman. Primary DMD staffers involved in canal redevelopment include John Klipsch, Dave Whitcher, Larry Coffey, Mike Perry, Harold Rominger, Paula Whitney, Bob Wilch, Steve Schulmeyer, and Peggy Frazier.

[133] Indianpolis Board of Public Works Resolution No. 2437, Oct. 13, 1980; Quitclaim Deed and Instrument of Transfer of Easement and Other Rights, Oct. 15, 1980 (Baker and Daniels Legal Archives, Indianapolis).

[134] Krannert Charitable Trust and IWC pledged two private gifts for renovation. White River State Park engaged James Associates as the pumphouse design consultants, hired the contractor, and supervised renovation.

[135] Sasaki Design Team designed the project for the U.S. Army Corps of Engineers, Louisville District, and the White River Park Commision.

[136] Indianapolis *Star*, February 5, 2000.

[137] The map was created with "ThinkMap" computer software by Indianapolis consulting engineer Steve Letterman of WTH Engineering, in cooperation with Canal Society of Indiana vice president Chuck Huppert, local historians Jerry Sargent and Joe McClung, and the author.

Printed in the United States
20614LVS00003B/404

9 781403 339126